Journal for Architecture and Literature

# #6

# City Narratives as Places of Meaningfulness, Appropriation and Integration

Edited by

Sonja Novak

Susana Oliveira

Angeliki Sioli

Klaske Havik

nai010 publishers

cost EUROPEAN COOPERATION IN SCIENCE & TECHNOLOGY

writing urban places

CONTENT

# *Becoming Part of...* City Narratives as Places of Meaningfulness, Appropriation and Integration

**Sonja Novak, Angeliki Sioli, Susana Oliveira and Klaske Havik**

'You become part of the street, the neighbourhood, the city, the country, so perfectly, so delicately aligned, assimilated, that you disappear,' reads the excerpt from the pages of Edmund de Waal's latest book, *Letters to Camondo* (2021), an epistolary illustrated novel of sorts.[1] De Waal empathically uncovers the meanings of assimilation in a very particular context, portraying a Jewish family established in a big house in late nineteenth-century Paris with all its exquisite as well as tragic vicissitudes.

In spite of these specific circumstances, the quote, and the novel more generally, highlight how the built environment can absorb us, integrate us and incorporate us to such an extent that we seamlessly become a meaningful part of it. In that way it poignantly echoes the themes of meaningfulness, appropriation and integration that form the focus of this issue of *Writingplace*. In fact, these terms have been identified in the current EU COST Action Network Writing Urban Places, as points of departure for approaching, engaging with and intervening in mid-size European cities. Within this Action Network, these terms are understood in a specific way. Meaningfulness is seen as offering urban communities and spatial agents (architects, urbanists, designers and planners, among others) the instruments and methods to interpret their environment and thus their tasks and engagements towards that environment as a whole. Experiential, collective and personal, historical and site-specific qualities of space attribute meaning and identity to urban places. Therefore, meaningfulness can be explored through historical narratives, oral history and cultural heritage in the (re)construction of urban identities. Appropriation is the possibility to act and empower local communities, by improving their ability to project feelings and expectations on urban planning schemes and built environment strategies. The role of local actors (users, inhabitants and other stakeholders) becomes crucial in such urban processes, precisely because they are the ones who experience and develop their surroundings and local conditions. Lastly, integration is seen as offering concrete tools and methods for the construction of common grounds among diverse and often contrasting communities, allowing for multiple narratives, embodiments, and urban developments to interact and connect, creating new meanings and appropriations of space.

Within this frame of reference, we invited submissions of original research papers that, from an inter- or a multidisciplinary theoretical perspective, attempt to define and illustrate meaningfulness, appropriation and integration in the context of mid-size European cities. The proposals were expected to explore narratives and stories of meaningfulness in the urban environment, examples of urban appropriation from different local agents, architectural processes and literary perspectives on community integration in the European urban context. COST members of the Writing Urban Places Action were purposefully invited to contribute, and to team up with one or more members of the COST Network.

The disappearing of the subject in De Waal's literary description above seems to allude to integration with the urban surroundings, not as a form of dissolution into non-existence, but, on the contrary, as an image of deep understanding and engagement with the urban environment and its aspects. The articles collected in this issue attempt a similar alignment with their places, subjects, perceptions and stories, while describing, in their assemblage, a miscellaneous tour guiding us from Oxford to Ghent, from

Naples to Sheffield, and from Riga to some historical towns in Spain. Along this journey across Europe, with a small detour to Latin America, the articles discuss, in relation to our core concepts, issues of inclusivity, politics, urban heritage, collective housing, agency and activism.

This issue of *Writingplace* was preceded by an online symposium with the same title, organized by Working Group 2 of the COST Action Network Writing Urban Places in November 2020. This event was an attempt to get a step closer to determining these terms from a theoretical perspective. As we noticed both during the symposium and the editorial work on this issue, the three themes are by no means mutually exclusive. As Sonja Novak and Angeliki Sioli stated in their reflection on the symposium:

> *Interestingly enough, the last of the three listed terms – integration – seems to ironically have the tendency to question any type of setting boundaries as its definition and the main idea behind it is to incorporate something into a larger unit; to form, coordinate or blend into a functioning or unified whole; it refers to desegregation and is thus a paradox that is proving quite difficult to define from a theoretical point of view.*[2]

This issue is therefore an invitation to look beyond the definitions of meaningfulness, appropriation and integration, and explore the relations between them. We have liberally arranged the articles under the three main themes but, as it can easily become clear, there are overlaps among the themes. In that way, this issue offers not only a geographical journey along different urban narratives, but also an expedition into the network of interrelated terms and spatial practices.

*Writingplace* #6 opens with a piece on urban landscape, contributed by Saskia de Wit, who presents a walk through Oxford, a mid-size European city with a strong identity. Weaving the landscape of the non-traditional architectural ensemble of St Catherine's College into that of the historical urban landscape, this paper aims to unfold the physical landscape – and the way it is perceived – as a generator of meaningfulness. According to De Wit, this ensemble exposes just how much the quality of the physical landscape can affect what we perceive and how we attach meanings to what we perceive.

Indeed, meaning may be generated through our embodied perception – as De Wit makes clear – as well as through the narratives that are entangled with urban environments. Kris Pint's article 'Narrative Deserts and Embodied Meanings in the City' also touches on the embodied experience of urban and architectural elements – in this case the Stadshal (City Pavilion) in Ghent – and discusses this experience in relation to the microstories of Ghent's City Pavilion. Taking that particular architectural project as an example, Pint addresses Michel de Certeau's notions of narrativity of space and their juxtaposition with the technocratic and economic discourse of efficiency and homogenization of contemporary cities. He also examines Mark Johnson's idea of emerging meaningfulness as a formative force. As comes to the fore in Pint's contribution, meaningfulness is inseparably connected to language and communication, whose main purpose is to convey a literal or symbolic message or create an atmosphere.

Giuseppe Resta's article 'The Belly of Naples and Displaced Meanings' employs the tropes of city-as-body and city-as-theatre to examine selected literary representations of the city of Naples in the late-nineteenth-century *Risanamento* period, a period that was characterized by dramatic renovations of the old town. The departure work of reference is *Il Ventre di Napoli* (1884) by writer and journalist Matilde Serao. Resta analyses how Serao tackles the contradictions of a built environment by means of bodily metaphors, in parallel with excerpts from foreign travelers of the same time-period such as Charles Dickens, and later visitors like Jean-Paul Sartre and Walter Benjamin. They all deconstruct the stereotype of the picturesque and displaced meaning, which allows Resta to understand and defy the formation of stereotypical images associated with the picturesque of the South, through the example of Naples.

For the next article, we remain in Naples and gradually move into the theme of appropriation by looking at a representation of the city from a feminist perspective. Sernaz Arslan's study 'Appropriation and Gender Spaces: A Discussion on Elena Ferrante's Neapolitan Novels' looks into the famous tetralogy that narrates the lives of two female friends within the strict and limiting confines of their lower-class neighbourhood. The space of the neighbourhood, but parts of the rest of the city as well, are appropriated in ways that change as the women grow and the sociopolitical conditions of the country (and Europe) transition and advance. Arslan's article explores how the female characters interact with and experience the urban space, while her reading sheds light on issues of gender and class as connected with the conversation on appropriation.

Expanding on the perspective of women, we follow Dalia Milián Bernal, who takes us far from the European continent to present the stories of appropriation of vacant and abandoned urban spaces by four women in the city of San Juan, Puerto Rico. By means of narrative inquiry, and based conceptually on Lefebvre's notion of appropriation, her article 'Narratives of Appropriation: Abandoned Spaces, Entangled Stories, and Profound Urban Transformations', collects and presents the individual and collective efforts of these women to transform and give new uses to these spaces. At the same time, it shows how these women assert their right to the city, caring for an active participation in the processes of urbanization. The article concludes by discussing how the women's actions might have inspired and encouraged similar processes elsewhere and might have planted seeds for future practice-based processes and research.

Continuing on the notion of appropriation, and building upon selected writings by Henri Lefebvre as well, Nevena Novaković's article 'The Concept of

Appropriation in Collective Housing Design: Understanding Dwelling as a Poetic Practice' provides a contribution to the ongoing theoretical debate on collective housing design by focusing on dwelling as a poetic practice. Novaković defends the methodological potential of appropriation as a concept that fosters the understanding of dwelling. The author looks into dwelling as the creative practice of human fulfillment, meaning an analytical tool for reading the transformation of existing space by its inhabitants.

While the articles in the section of appropriation bring to the fore the perspectives of particular user groups, the next set of articles discusses how different social groups can come together, acknowledging that spatial integration is behavioural: it is a quality towards the built environment of accepting, adapting, transforming the place but also other people's ideas, mentalities and sociospatial practices. Based on a recently finished research project that involved ordinary objects of minor villages and towns from the Valencia Region in Southern Spain, Juan Garcia Esparza's contribution discusses how assessing and discussing everyday artifacts can improve conservation practices, taking into account the inhabitants' experience of their town. His article 'Narrating the Urban Fabric of Our Historical Towns' explores informal expressions of cultural heritage in historical towns, and analyses new forms of appraisal in historical urban settlements. The suggested approach challenges the idealistic constructed scenarios of the past and creates space for new interpretations on the cultural diversity of the unplannable or informal place-making. In doing so, it examines how historical values can better incorporate past and contemporary anthropological informalities.

While integration can be stimulated by more inclusive approaches to urban analysis, it is as important to examine how integration is obstructed, and how spatial and social obstructions can be challenged. Dace Bula's article 'Sites of Narrativity and Spatial Debate: Fences in Neighbourhoods in the Port of Riga' examines, through an ethnographical approach, how fences surrounding urban public spaces can be perceived as 'storied', that is, possessing the quality of being and/or producing narratives. Through examples from the case study of the Riga port and the four areas around the estuary of the Daugava River, the author shows how the residents react to the newly introduced fences of their surroundings that seem to exclude and separate them rather than integrate and include them. The paper attempts to bridge narrative and material studies by exploring the ways the imposed fences fragment the residents' built environment. This fragmentation urges them to construct their own nostalgic and activist narratives, along with narratives pertaining to everyday practical life, like how one accesses the waterfront or the difficulties they face getting from one place to another.

Finally, the article 'Beyond Community: Inclusivity through Spatial Interventions' by Asma Mehan, Krzysztof Nawratek and Farouq Tahar argues against the concept of integration as the main mechanism that allows various sociocultural groups to live together. Instead, the authors propose 'radical inclusivity' as a less oppressive model for a pluralistic society. Through analytical and reflective research on the non-cohesion-based approach to integration or inclusion, this article examines the affordances and limitations of integration through various forms of spatial interventions. The authors discuss the case study of the Ellesmere Green Project in Sheffield (UK) as a typical small urban regeneration executed in a highly diverse part of the city. This piece thus aims to bring forward the significance of moving beyond the community-as-cohesion model in urban politics and planning for integration.

Instead of providing a holistic definition of each of the terms – meaningfulness, appropriation and integration – the articles in this issue of *Writingplace* demonstrate that these terms cannot be analysed or defined as independent, but rather as open and interconnected. Meaningfulness is in itself a notion that implies a fullness of relation between form and content, where form can be either permanent or ephemeral, physical or intangible and the content literal or symbolic. It is the process of integration of the two that further adds meaning. In both individual and collective observations as well as subjective processing of what we consider meaning, we appropriate these ideas by adding our own input. Indeed, appropriation – positive or negative connotations aside – inevitably includes a kind of change or transformation. This, in turn, creates new meanings that vary according to the different scales, from that of the individual, to the local community and the social group, all the way to the region.

There is a clear need for multiperspectivity in understanding meaningfulness, appropriation and integration but, in terms of impact and scale, the articles have shown how the mid-size European city is an ideal context to examine these terms. The mid-size city 'can serve as a useful lens in describing a broad section of the European continent'[3] and it is also a fruitful starting point to explore the tendencies of contemporary urban environments with all their narratives.

It is exactly this relation between the terms meaningfulness, appropriation and integration and the scale of the mid-size European cities that shifts the emphasis to the people of a given place. The mid-size scale allows the city's inhabitants to act as different stakeholders in the processes of urban and societal development. They are not overwhelmed or absorbed by the massiveness of a metropolis. Thus, they are easier motivated to search for creation of meanings, appropriation and integration of certain places in the built urban environment. They become part of the stories of their own place.

1 Edmund De Waal, *Letters to Camondo* (London, 2021), 152.

2 Some fragments in this editorial were adapted from the report of the on-line mini conference 'Meaningfulness, Appropriation and Integration of/in City Narratives, organized by Sonja Novak and Angeliki Sioli, Working group 2 of the COST Action Network *Writing Urban Places*, in November 2020. The pdf – including links to the recording of this event – is available at: writingurbanplaces.eu/output/meaningfulness-appropriation-and-integration-of-in-city-narratives/

3 See: Michiel Dehaene, Bruno Notteboom and Klaske Havik, 'Medium: The Mid-Size City as a European Urban Condition and Strategy', *OASE* 89 (2013), 2-9.

# *A Walk to the Cherwell River Meadows* (Meaningfulness and) the Perceivable Form of the Urban Landscape

**Saskia de Wit**

'If there can be no form without meaning, there can be no meaning without form,' wrote architect Steven Kent Peterson when discussing the value of defined architectural space.[1] Approaching the transaction between people and the urban landscape as one of affective relationships is about the perceiver as much as about the perceived. In contemporary literature on our relationship with the urban environment, the focus has shifted from object to subject and agency, and thus from information to information seeking, from the production to the reception of sensory stimuli.[2] However, I would like to contend here that meaningfulness is not primarily an asset of the perceiver, but of the perceived: the urban landscape as a reservoir of possible meanings. We derive meaning from or attribute meaning to things, spaces, territories, based on our experiences. And experiences are localized: 'All experiences – smells, sounds, weight, temperature, texture – are localized in one perceptual space,' as Malnar and Vodvarka argued.[3]

In order to arrive at some insights on the role of perceivable form, I will take you on an excursion to Oxford, a mid-size European city with a strong urban identity. So strong, indeed, that although alternative interpretations are possible, they tend to end up outside the major narratives of town and gown, 'dreaming spires', picturesque cityscape and Harry Potter-esque mystery. By weaving the landscape of the non-traditional architectural ensemble of St Catherine's College into that of the traditional urban landscape, this paper aims to unfold (the perception of) the physical landscape, beyond the polemics of architectural style, as a generator of meaningfulness. Devoid of the style characteristics that determine our mental image of Oxford, but remaining loyal to the programmatic and compositional logic of the Oxford colleges, the ensemble exposes just how much the quality of the physical landscape can affect what we perceive and how we attach meanings to what we perceive.

### A Modern College in Oxford

St Catherine's College was designed between 1959 and 1964 by Danish architect Arne Jacobsen. It is built on a river island just outside Oxford city centre, in the floodplains of the River Cherwell. A raised plateau provides a canvas on which the building ensemble is symmetrically organized around a central axis. The college is broken up into volumes, spaced wide apart to let space flow unhindered between them. The height of the buildings does not exceed three storeys, as high as many older colleges, but their distance to each other makes them appear lower, creating a horizontality that responds to the landscape horizon. Only the bell tower rises like a single vertical. This belltower is placed in a separate courtyard, not affecting the spatial form of the quadrangle, like the vertical towers, gates and chapels in the traditional colleges.

Not only did Jacobsen transpose the traditional typology into a modern idiom, he also transposed the urban typology of the college onto the open river landscape, opening up the spatial composition without corrupting the basic central organization of the college type. It is this aspect of opening up to the landscape, more than the architectural style, that is rather revolutionary for this traditional English town.

> *Within a traditional urban-landscape dichotomy there would have been two choices for this river meadow location: to incorporate the site into the urban fabric or to preserve it as an open landscape. Instead, the design reflects equally the urban and the landscape conditions, giving room to local qualities and highlighting the possibilities of the open landscape as an integral part of the urban landscape.*[6]

The arrangement of elements such as enclosing wall, staircase, gate, tower and quadrangle forges a new relationship between town and countryside, acting as devices of mediation that guide movement and provoke a layering of uses and meanings.

**Walking in Oxford**

In the period the college was built, architects, urban designers and landscape architects experimented with ways of analysis and design that took the narrative, spatiotemporal perspective of the experiencing subject moving through the city as the starting point, in a response to what was perceived as an estranged and abstract perspective of modernist urban planning. Among them was architect Peter Smithson. In a 1976 article, he identified Oxford as:

> *A lexicon of mediators in the language of architecture . . . enclosing wall, turreted gateway, snicket, cloister, passage, screens passage, stair, set-door. All devices of mediation – between open street and closed quadrangle; between quadrangle of one quality and quadrangle of*

> *another; between communal quadrangle and communal hall or chapel; between communal passage, cloister, or quadrangle, and personal room.*[4]

He explained these 'separate *words* in the language of architecture in this lexicon', as architectural inventions ('the legs-in-the-air multiple-field space of Tudor architecture'), transposed onto the urban fabric.

But his interest did not lie in the words themselves:

> *In Oxford the clamour of actual answering turrets is very strong – caused in part by the irregular arrangement of the streets which makes one see the same ranks and clusters of turrets and chimneys, field beyond field, many times over – like a stage army. And there is also the crowding; the closeness and the jostling of the buildings.*[5]

The words begin to make sense when strung together in a visual sequence, seen from an eye-level perspective: the crowding and the visual layering do not manifest in a map. It seems as if these elements and their relationships, 'that multiple-field architectural space which is so special to Oxford', can only be properly described from the perspective of the pedestrian, and thus the core of Smithson's article reads like a tourist guide, carefully describing five different walks though Oxford and Cambridge. The physical landscape – its devices of mediation, and their arrangement in relation to one another – is not a two-dimensional or even three-dimensional structure, but can only be grasped when time is also included, the time it takes to move through the city, as a spatiotemporal continuity.

Peter Smithson must have walked right past St Catherine's College, but he fully ignored its existence. The architectural language of modernism and the English Renaissance multiple-field space that he so admired seem to have very distinct, even opposite, conceptions of architectural space, and St Catherine's clean and modern appearance apparently did not fit his narrative of the typical Oxford fabric, a narrative of cluttering and layer-

Fig. 1. Visual score of the original route from Oxford city centre to St Catherine's College, as a layered sequence of devices of mediation, spaces and lines, views and landmarks.

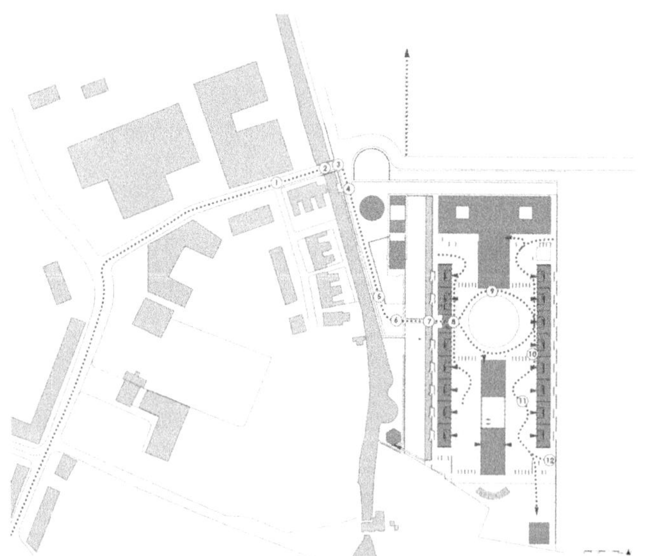

Fig. 2. The route from Oxford city centre to St Catherine's College.

ing and transitioning. However, when one allows for multiple readings, for meaningfulness rather than meaning, the college only adds to the layered narrative of the Oxford townscape.

**Walking through St Catherine's College**

Only a few bridges cross the River Cherwell. Magdalen Bridge connects Oxford city centre to the eastern part of the city, the only place where the Cherwell is exposed to the city. Five hundred metres north of Magdalen Bridge is the small Nappers Bridge, not crossing the Cherwell, but leading to the river island between the Cherwell and Holywell Mill Stream. Walking across Nappers Bridge, one's eye is drawn over the length of the stream towards St Catherine's belltower, guiding the visitor along the banks of the stream. The river walk passes a circular bicycle shed and leads to an entrance square, where it turns away from the stream to face the building. First to catch the eye is the unambiguous image of modern architecture.

> *Nowhere in Oxford is there a stronger sense of a modern university as a secular, essentially utilitarian institution, and nowhere in England is there a purer statement of the architectural ideas of the Modern Movement as understood in its heroic earlier years.*[7]

Instead of the enclosed spaces of the traditional colleges, buildings and garden elements appear as a simple and legible composition, built out of clearly discernible basic geometric shapes, and grouped in an arrangement of volumes on a single orthogonal grid. The continuity of space is expressed in the horizontality of building volumes and façades. In the façades the construction is expressed in a pronounced rhythm, and the concrete frames project through the brick walls at ground level, giving them a sculptural quality.

This modern visual image is counteracted by the sounds and smells of waterfowl. A lawn – marked by Barbara Hepworth's bronze sculpture

Fig. 3. Façade of St Catherine's College, as seen from entrance square: a clean and modern façade, above a sculptural and interwoven edge of land and water, building and site, architecture and landscape.

Fig. 4. The quadrangle of St Catherine's College presents a static image of order, clarity and immutability.

*Achaean* (1959) – and a canal-shaped pool mark the boundary of the rectangular plateau. In contrast to the clean geometry of the building façade, this edge between plateau and lawn is an elaborated brick wall with niches and buttresses, providing ample space for free-growing shrubs and weeds. This rich transition zone between water and land, architecture and nature, designed and unexpected, provides an architecturally defined waterscape for ducks, geese, herons and moorhen. A narrow footbridge, almost at water level, leads across lawn and pool towards the glass façade of the western wing, where the quadrangle is glimpsed through the glass walls of the foyer. The entrance itself is a simple hole pierced in the continuing building volume, a discreet passage typical for Oxford colleges.

The quadrangle, with its circular lawn and majestic (evergreen) cedar tree, presents a static image of order, clarity and immutability, unchanging whether one is walking or standing still, in summer or winter. From the quadrangle one can choose to go either to one of the staircases that lead to the student study-bedrooms, or, through the gardens, to the other parts of the college.

A series of alternating hedges and freestanding walls, supporting a light roof, connect the quadrangle to four gardens. Here, the pattern of movement opens up into a leisurely meandering around plant beds and lawns, connecting not only a range of destinations, but also allowing for a range of possible routes to one's destination. In contrast to the quadrangle, the walk through the gardens will be quite different depending on the season, with spring-flowering magnolias and camellias in May and June, and autumn berries and the fierce red leaves of Japanese maples in October and November, to coincide with the seasonality of the academic year.
A profusion of plants creates variation within the unifying framework of the gridded floor. The impressionistic series of planting compositions functions as an incentive to move forward, but without a precise agenda

Fig. 5. In contrast to the quadrangle, the gardens of St Catherine's College are an intimate and intricate fabric of planting and paving, changing through the seasons.

Fig. 6. Balcony of St Catherine's College, looking out over the Merton College recreation ground and the forested river shores.

or defined stages leading to a climax, which provides a more improvisational and personalized understanding of the spaces.

Having crossed the gardens, one reaches the edge of the plateau, beyond the accommodation wings. The plateau is like a balcony, affording a view back over the lawn and the pool, or to the other side over the Merton College recreation ground and the forested river shores. Since this balcony is hidden behind the buildings, one could easily move around the college without ever catching a glimpse of these meadows. Yet, the atmosphere of the river land-scape is omnipresent. The coolness of the air, the scent of freshness and the sounds of waterfowl – the sensory components of the rural landscape – permeate the college. More than the visual, the auditory and olfactory aspects firmly place the college in the rural landscape of the river meadows.

The appearance of these meadows has not changed much since Georgian times, despite their gradual transformation into the current recreational pro-gramme. The interventions in size, shape, enclosure and material (a grass floor) were minimal. Some meadows are used as public parks, recognizable only from the garbage bins; otherwise they look exactly like the pasture they used to be. If you know where to look, you can reach these fields, as access is provided by a barely visible footpath that branches off from the entrance road. The path connects to the network of public footpaths, bicycle paths and bridleways that criss-cross along the Cherwell. The paths are hidden in the tree-lined edges of the fields and only become visible when a high and slim footbridge crosses the Cherwell. They form an informal and hardly vis-ible yet densely knit connection between the sports fields and the public and collective parks.

**Connecting City and Countryside**

Although the college is situated in the fields, it is the connection to the urban network that is self-evident. The spatial organization is reminiscent of sequences within the traditional city, such as New College with its axial sequence and its central lawn, and Radcliffe Square with its open corners. And while the college directly borders the Cherwell, its boathouse, shared with other colleges, sits on the River Thames. Other college functions – playing fields, chapel and some college flats – are also scattered across the city. This creates an intense movement pattern through town, specifically used by St Catherine's residents.

At the same time, almost unnoticeably, the river meadows are introduced: in the transition from the simple planting with indigenous trees at the edges of the plateau, via the lush gardens, to the abstracted image of grass and the monumental tree in the quadrangle. Visually the fields participate in the urban routing, as a subtle endpoint, and smell and sound of the river meadows permeate the outdoor space of the college.

City and river meadows both have fine-meshed, dense and irregular patterns of paths, but with their own internal logic, and the links between them are not easy to find. Urban morphology, programme and routing coincide in the urban network; the rural pattern is looser and broader, overlaid on the agricultural pattern. The connection to the rural network is informal and only for those who know where to look, maintaining a separation between urban and rural network. The college acts as the mediation between city and fields: more specifically the quadrangle, the traffic hub of the college, with a vital role in the obligations and regulations of active daily life.

The modernist idiom of clearly defined built objects in a spatial continuum is transformed into a multiple-field space by the use of planting, which forms interlocking spaces. Aided by these spatial determinants the central quadrangle mediates between the dense urban fabric and the broad yet delineated landscape space of the river meadows. It does so by combining the spatial and sensory characteristics of the open river landscape with those of the college, familiarizing both. The quadrangle is the pivot point: a fixed moment of immobility in the spatial sequence that links the college to the

Fig. 7. St Catherine's College, immersed in the presence of the river.
All colour photo's by Saskia de Wit.

Fig. 8. St Catherine's College, succession of different specimens of the cedar tree in the quadrangle in 55 years: the original *Cedrus libani* in 1966, planted as a mature tree; the *Cedrus atlantica* 'Glauca' in 2005 with a diagonal branching structure, just before it was removed, its successor already waiting on its left; and the newly planted *Cedrus libani* in 2011, still a chubby little ball.

city centre, and the outward-oriented organization of space of the college to the meadow. By thus mediating between city and river landscape in this indirect and informal manner reminiscent of the way the architectural mediators work in the urban fabric, the college presents its mixed message of urbanity and rurality, old and new, definition and freedom.

**Changing Form**

The spatial sequence described above is what Peter Smithson might have experienced in 1976, had he not averted his eyes from the modernist architecture. It is not, however, what the current pedestrian would see. In 1982 the original routing along the stream was superseded by a revised routing, necessitated by the addition of new buildings at the north end of the scheme. The present route leads straight ahead from Nappers Bridge to the new Porter's Lodge. From here one continues through the service buildings and the gardens, to arrive at the quadrangle from the north, bypassing the sequence of interlocking spaces, views and landmarks.

The composition of the gardens remains mostly unaltered, although most of the original trees and shrubs have been replaced, most notably the prominent cedar tree in the quadrangle. The Cedar of Lebanon *(Cedrus libani)* was chosen, according to Jacobsen, to produce 'the most powerful horizontal effect possible, entirely emphasizing and continuing the design of the architecture.'[8] Narrow and pyramidal in their youth, in their adult state the branches of these trees are set wide apart in expressive horizontal planes. The first specimen, however, had been replanted from a neighbouring garden as an adult tree and was slowly dying. In 1972 a second tree was planted, to the right of the original one, in order to eventually replace it.
This turned out to be the wrong species: the blue-leaved *Cedrus atlantica* 'Glauca' with more diagonal branches. So now a third one, still young, has replaced the blue cedar, maybe one day presenting the intended impressive effect, but right now a chubby little ball, not forming the space, but an object in space.

Did the meaning of the quadrangle change over time, between one cedar tree and the next? Do those who pass through the quadrangle appreciate or understand what Jacobsen intended? Does it even matter whether they do? Jane Gillette suggests that 'the actuality [of the physical landscape] and its effect on our senses is more important than its maker's message, should there have been one. Yes, in time meaning may ensue but it is probably not the meaning intended by the maker.'[9] Meaning is ultimately personal, and probably more derived 'from our cultural matrix paired with personal experience, knowledge and feelings.' However, since the stimulus to our readings, that which is perceived, has changed, the meanings we derive from it change as well.

**Conclusion**

Thus, the main concern when approaching and intervening in mid-sized European cities is not whether inhabitants or visitors consciously perceive what is there to be perceived, and consequently what meanings they derive from the urban environment – as an asset of the perceiver – but to unearth what it is that the physical landscape holds – as an asset of the perceived, the *perceivable form* of the urban landscape. The focus should shift to the qualities of the perceived: the physical surroundings as carriers of multiple meanings, shifting and evolving over time.

Meaningfulness in the urban landscape is guided by (sensory) perception: the qualities of the environment only become meaningful if they can be experienced, and they can only be experienced when possible experiences are structured, served and enhanced by perceivable form. Form (which includes materiality as well as structure) provides the conditions of experience. Sensory qualities are inherent attributes of the physical environment, which can serve as a stimulus or catalyst for the meanings/meaningfulness each of us derives from or attributes to the environment. The elements of the urban landscape, the separate *words* in the language of architecture, provide not images with a defined meaning, but bodily perceivable kinaesthetic events that allow each urban dweller or visitor to create his or her own narrative. A narrative that only begins to make sense when the words, those kinaesthetic events, are strung together in a perceptual sequence, in mutual, spatiotemporal relationships. As Eugene Victor Walter writes: 'A place is a location of experience. It evokes and organizes memories, images, feelings, sentiments, meanings and the work of imagination. The feelings of a place are indeed the mental projections of individuals, but they come from collective experience and they do not happen anywhere else. They belong to the place.'[10]

1 Steven Kent Peterson, 'Space and Anti-Space', *Harvard Architecture Review* (spring 1980), 88-113.
2 Dolores Hayden, *The Power of Place: Urban Landscapes as Public History* (Cambridge, MA, 1995), a.o.
3 Joy Monice Malnar and Frank Vodvarka, *Sensory Design* (Minneapolis, 2004), 45.
4 Peter Smithson, 'Oxford and Cambridge Walks', *Architectural Design* (1976), 332.
5 Ibid., 335.
6 Saskia de Wit, *Hidden Landscapes: The Metropolitan Garden as a Multi-Sensory Expression of Place* (Amsterdam, 2018), 195-196.
7 Geoffrey Tyack, *Oxford: An Architectural Guide* (Oxford/New York, 1998), 310.
8 Arne Jacobsen in an interview by Ole Dreyer in the programme 'Arne Jacobsen in Oxford', Danish Broadcasting Corporation, 1969. Cited in: Carsten Thau and Kjelt Vindum, *Jacobsen* (Copenhagen, 2000), 482-483.
9 Marc Treib, *Meaning in Landscape Architecture & Gardens* (Abingdon/New York, 2011), xvii.
10 Eugene Victor Walter, *Placeways: A Theory of the Human Environment* (Chapel Hill, NC, 1988), 21.

# *Narrative Deserts and Embodied Meanings in the City*

## The Microstories of Ghent's City Pavilion

**Kris Pint**

### Meaningfulness in a Narrative Desert: Violent, Vital Microstories

Many urban environments seem to suffer from what architecture theorist Françoise Choay calls 'semantic reduction' or *hyposignifiance*, with only one form of meaning left: the economic discourse of production and consumption.[1] This creates what we could call narrative deserts: spaces without a thriving narrative ecosystem that provides sufficient different, meaningful stories to its inhabitants. In *The Practice of Everyday Life* (1980) Michel de Certeau paints a similar picture:

> *Where stories are disappearing (or else are being reduced to museographical objects), there is a loss of space: deprived of narrations (as one sees it happen in both the city and the countryside), the group or the individual regresses toward the disquieting, fatalistic experience of a formless, indistinct, and nocturnal totality.*[2]

In de Certeau's dystopian view, the suppression of stories and legends by a technocratic and economic discourse of efficiency and homogenization makes the contemporary city uninhabitable. Historical narratives and cultural meanings are often reduced to elements of touristic city branding, without as much as a vital link to the actual daily life of city dwellers.

> *Thus, as a woman from Rouen puts it, no, here 'there isn't any place special, except for my own home, that's all . . . . There isn't anything.' Nothing 'special': nothing that is marked, opened up by a memory or a story, signed by something or someone else. Only the cave of the home remains believable, still open for a certain time to legends, still full of shadows. Except for that, according to another city-dweller, there are only 'places in which one can no longer believe in anything'.*[3]

However, the strong sense of melancholy in de Certeau's analysis is countered by a belief in a tactical form of resistance: the proliferation of meaningful practices, creating microstories that stubbornly resist the spatial and discursive homogenization promoted by mass media, marketing and politics. The proliferation of these microstories provides the inhabitants with 'spatial trajectories' and helps them to give meaning to their everyday life. Like public transport, these minor stories allow individuals to escape the reductive, controlling and fixating strategies of a technocratic society that only addresses them in their economic role as potential consumer or producer. Seen from this perspective, an apparent narrative desert can actually be full of such hidden storylines. A good example is urban photographer Jeff Mermelstein's *#nyc* (2020), a series that captures the text messages of New Yorker's smartphones in public spaces.[4] The results are narrative fragments of desire and despair, gossip and advice that add a multitude of layers to urban places and trajectories.

More than 40 years after its first publication in France, de Certeau's investigation is still relevant to the discussion of meaningfulness and urbanism.

It holds a warning against the potential danger of contemporary concepts like 'smart cities' (even with the best intentions, for example fighting climate change). Such an approach runs the risk of repeating the errors of the past, of making the same arrogant mistake modernist urbanists and experts made in thinking they could control the city and its microstories. These narrative practices continue to challenge any interpretative framework that tries to recuperate these practices; and resist any effort to be assimilated into a technocratic spatial regime:

> *Totalitarianism attacks what it quite correctly calls superstitions: supererogatory semantic overlays that insert themselves 'over and above' and 'in excess' and annex to a past or poetic realm a part of the land the promoters of technical rationalities and financial profitabilities had reserved for themselves.*[5]

Certeau's idea of stories that resist the urban technocracy was indebted to the surrealist and situationist movements of twentieth-century France, as well as to the student and workers' protests of May '68. What they had in common was the exploration of other modes of existence, other 'ways of operating' within the structures of production and consumption that dominate the modern city. But in the age of post-truth and fake news, Paris Spring slogans like 'l'imagination au pouvoir' have now acquired a sinister undertone. Michel de Certeau was right: stories and legends can never be fully erased, and in contemporary society a great deal of the population seems to feel lost in a kind of fearful 'nocturnal totality', desperately searching for stories to believe in, for a narrative shape to make sense of a formless everyday existence.

So while for Certeau 'superstition' is a positive term, the past decades also showed the destructive nature of some of these stories that challenge modernity: from the rise of religious fundamentalism, to the reactivation of conspiracy theories that seem primitive in their medieval imaginary of Satanic cults, with a malignant elite poisoning the population, using chemtrails and vaccines. These 'superstitions' travel the same way as the microstories captured by Mermelstein's camera, through the virtual space of social media. They, too, are 'spatial trajectories' into the parallel, virtual 'polis' of the Internet, mostly invisible for those not in the same 'virtual bubble'. People sitting next to you on a bus or train may be in the same actual place, but the narrative space accessed through their mobile devices might be radically different.

A revealing event in this case is the storming by a violent mob of the United States Capitol on 6 January 2021. The stories that led up to this bizarre attempt at a coup were clearly 'in excess', incited by 'semantic overlays' of a 'past realm', in this case, the historical narrative of the Civil War, with the prominent use of confederate flags. It showed that this need for meaning as a way to defy and resist technocratic functionalism can also generate violent and destructive counterstories.

This is a danger that is inherent to the linguistic nature of narratives. Ferdinand de Saussure's analysis of language made clear that meaning is not so much a question of reference, of establishing a kind of correct, truthful relationship with the outside world, but a question of differences within a linguistic system itself, not only on the level of form (for example the difference between sounds that generate a difference in meaning), but also on the level of content. A differing other is always needed to determine an element's meaning: it is the distinctive difference that allows meaning to appear. Meaningfulness requires a form of opposition, of 'othering', to work. In the Christian framework of de Certeau – a Jesuit – this 'othering' has a positive connotation: it is the promise that any given structure or system is never fixed and can always be opened up, transformed for the better.[6] But in many stories the other appears as an opponent, as an unwelcome enemy. Here one can think of Greimas's actantial model as the abstract blueprint of every story: with an opposition between the subject, the protagonist, who wants something else, an object, and who has helpers and opponents, with again conflicting interests.[7] As Greimas makes clear, the creation of meaning in stories, both fictional and non-fictional, is by definition antagonistic, based on radical differences, and thus inherently conflictual and potentially violent.

It is important to keep in mind this oppositional structure when we analyse not only the stories of dwellers of specific urban areas, but also the metastories of researchers, spatial professionals and policymakers (in de Certeau's story of modern life 'the promoters of technical rationalities and financial profitabilities' clearly take the oppositional role of the classic villain). If the narrative framework changes, the evaluation of the different actants changes as well, and the same actions can suddenly be perceived in a radically different, yet equally meaningful light. The attempt to re-evaluate the historical dimension of a site, the rich cultural heritage of a specific urban area can be very helpful to give meaning and generate a sense of pride for the local population. And yet it can also be 'read' as a shrewd, perhaps even cynical attempt to gentrify an area, to gradually push out lower-income households.

**Embodied Meanings, Affective Architecture: Ghent's City Pavilion**

The work of Michel de Certeau was strongly embedded in the (post)structuralist context of French theory. But recent decades saw the so-called affective or corporeal turn in the humanities, stressing the importance of sensual, affective experiences embedded in cultural artefacts, including architecture. An important book in this regard is Mark Johnson's *The Meaning of the Body: Aesthetics of Human Understanding* (2007). In this book, Johnson argues that our common understanding of meaning is much too focused on semantic, conceptual forms of meaning. In his previous work with Georg Lakoff, *Metaphors We Live By* (1980) and *Philosophy in the Flesh: The Embodied Mind and Its Challenge to Western Thought* (1999), Johnson already stressed the close, inseparable link between language and our understanding of the world. The language we use shapes our view of reality, but this language itself is shaped by bodily experiences. These form the sensorial, affective basis from which the more abstract concepts and images emerge with which we make sense of our environment. But for Johnson, these sensations and affects are in themselves already crucial in understanding the world. Meaningfulness is also produced by images, feelings, affects, emotions and kinaesthetic experiences, as well as by the sensual qualities of an atmosphere.[8]

Meaning is thus not so much the result of 'decoding' the text of our environment, but something that emerges in our embodied relation to and interaction with our environment. Meaning is not only propositional and language based, but can also be affective, emotional, sensorial. This is of course very relevant when we are talking about the meaning of architecture. The meaningfulness of a specific place does not only lie in the cultural, sociopolitical meanings it generates and the specific scripts and scenarios that are performed there. It can also be found in the specific bodily experiences the site makes possible, as crucial elements to give sense to a specific place. As Johnson argues in another text, 'The Embodied Meaning of Architecture' (2015), the role of architecture is to intensify this meaningful relationship with the environment:

> *My hypothesis is that architectural structures are experienced by humans as both sense-giving and signifying. That is, architectural structures present us, first, with a way of situating ourselves in, or being 'at home' in, and making sense of our world, and, second, they provide material and cultural affordances that are meaningful for our survival and flourishing as meaning-seeking creatures.*[9]

However, it is remarkable that just like de Certeau, Johnson seems to downplay the negative, and even violent, experiences that also produce embodied meanings. In his pragmatist view, our embodied relationship with our environment is holistic, harmonious, or at least strives for such harmony. But the actual relation to our environment is often less peaceful. Anxiety, anger and disgust can also be effective ways to give meaning to a specific environment, and are, whether we like it or not, part and parcel of everyday life – very much including our relation to the built environment.

As an example, I want to discuss the Stadshal, the City Pavilion (2012), right in the centre of Ghent, Belgium. The Pavilion was designed by Robbrecht & Daem and Marie-José Van Hee architects and quickly nicknamed the 'Schaapstal', the 'Sheep Stable'. The project was contested because it interfered with the historical nature of the square on which it was situated. Despite the obvious references to the surrounding medieval and renaissance buildings, the Pavilion looks brutally modern, and its massive size indeed obstructs part of the view.[10] It was initially also criticized by UNESCO because it was not consulted in the process. The expensive construction was also seen as an unnecessary prestige project, a waste of public money that was better spent on perhaps less spectacular, but more effective forms of urban development. It is, to paraphrase de Certeau, a site that is most definitely not 'deprived of narrations', including antagonistic ones, with as villains the arrogant politicians and architects. There is the interesting relationship between a modern city and its historical past, but also between tourists and locals, between the municipal authorities and some of the inhabitants of the city. Obviously, the Pavilion is used for city branding and the tourist industry. It is close to the commercial centre of Ghent's inner city, it has a 'grand café', and is easily integrated in the 'experience economy' of many European cities. Yet at the same time, the architectural features of the building also seem to resist this recuperation.

Partly, this is the result of Robbrecht & Daem and Marie-José Van Hee's paradoxical use of historical references. The design echoes the surrounding landscape and its cultural history, but at the same time feels like a brutal intrusion of a massive volume that does not blend in. We see the same approach in Robbrecht & Daem's Concert Hall in Bruges (1999-2002), and the refurbishment of some public squares in Deinze, also with Marie-José Van Hee (2009-2013), combining historical references with outspoken volumes and patterns. But the approach of the designers is only one way to oppose the dominance of an economic storyline. It also resides in the microstories that were 'performed' at this site in the past years, and which are not embedded in a larger commercial or political strategy, like the placing of some amateurishly made plush kittens in 2020 on the lawn before the Pavilion, or a spontaneous silent wake for a victim of a sex crime in 2021. These stories are transitory, and often do not go further than the regional newspaper, but they provide the kind of narrative anarchy that de Certeau found so necessary.

The City Pavilion is also a generator of embodied meanings. And again, the architectural qualities of the actual building play an important part. All of the meaningful features that Mark Johnson attributes to architecture are addressed. The building gives a sense of containment, shelter, and it also reinforces the very crucial senses of movement, verticality and gravity.[11] The gaze is directed upwards, towards the many small light wells in the wooden double roof, which leans together in the middle. The horizontal and diagonal lines of the canopy create a dynamism in the structure, while the sheer mass of the wooden construction and the concrete pedestals creates a sense of weight and grounds the building. On a sunny day, the shadows cast by this building are massive and abrupt, and you can follow their slow movement on the pavement, while the glass rooftiles reflect the sunlight, almost as if you are watching a very large, gravity-defying formal pond. There is also the visual rhyme with the forms of the windows, doors, roofs of the surrounding historical buildings, but always with a difference, a variation, foreclosing a too obvious harmony.

Of course, the actual use of the Pavilion also generates meaningful sensations: there is the rhythmical flow of people coming and going, the move-

Fig. 1. Market Hall, Ghent. Photograph by Peter Lorré.

ments made by users of the space for different events or activities, such as the performances and fairs that take place under this giant roof; there are children playing with each other, or people cycling underneath the canopy on a deserted and cold winter night; it can also give an emotional and physical sense of shelter, to escape a sudden summer rain shower. And despite its open and public character, it can even give one a sense of cosiness when the open fireplace in one of the concrete pedestals is occasionally lit.

A proper analysis of the meaning of the site would not be complete, however, without taking seriously the negative ones it also generates: in comparison with the other historical buildings and their refined medieval or renaissance façades, the Pavilion can look relentlessly heavy and stern. The massive roof and the huge, grey pedestals can feel depressing, literally and figuratively; the welcoming, open structure is strangely contradicted by its alien, uncompromising presence. Each time the square is approached, a sense of disgust, anger, sadness, or perhaps just a mild, but insisting frustration that the view is blocked might be experienced. And of course, the critique on this building should also be taken into account, its popular nickname of sheep stable, the microstories of people passing and commenting on the impact of the Pavilion: they, too, are fully part of the narrative landscape that is opened up by this building. The point is precisely that these negative bodily responses and microstories also give meaning to this space, just like the positive effects and sensations it creates: marking it as special, non-generic, quite opposite to the plain, unremarkable public parking lot it was before.

## Conclusion

The difficult question is, of course, what urbanists, designers and researchers' roles could and should be when faced with contemporary city lives and their messy, embodied multitude of meanings and stories. Perhaps the common task here can only be rather modest (albeit important): to explore and develop the narrative, meaningful 'affordances' of the built environment, and provide an ecosystem where different embodied meanings can thrive. Again, meanings that are embedded not only in stories, but also in embodied experiences, and in actual spatial trajectories: effects, emotions, senses. Meanings that go from bodily movements to atmospheres to bigger stories, linking the city both to a past and a future, and providing it with a viable narrative ecosystem that reduces 'hyposignifiance'. The underlying hypothesis here, following Johnson and de Certeau, is that if cities can create the economic, social conditions and the public space that allows for a vital thriving of meanings and stories, the narrative ecosystem might be vital and transformative enough to prevent one specific kind of destructive, negative stories and sensations from overgrowing the others.

1 André Loeckx and Hilde Heynen, 'Meaning and Effect: Revisiting Semiotics in Architecture', in: Sebastiaan Loosen, Rajesh Heynickx and Hilde Heynen (eds.), *The Figure of Knowledge. Conditioning Architectural Theory, 1960s–1990s* (Leuven, 2020), 31-61: 31-32.
2 Michel de Certeau, *The Practice of Everyday Life*, translated by Steven Rendall (Berkeley/Los Angeles/London, 1988), 123.
3 Ibid., 106.
4 Jeff Mermelstein, *#nyc* (London, 2020).
5 de Certeau, *The Practice of Everyday Life*, op. cit. (note 2), 106.
6 See: Michel de Certeau, *L'Etranger ou l'union dans la difference* (Paris, 2005).
7 Ronald Schleifer and Alan Velie, 'Genre and Structure: Toward an Actantial Typology of Narrative Genres and Modes', *MLN* 102/5 (1987), 1122-1150: 1126 ff.
8 Mark Johnson, *The Meaning of the Body: Aesthetics of Human Understanding* (Chicago, 2007), xi.
9 Mark Johnson, 'The Embodied Meaning of Architecture', in: Sarah Robinson and Juhani Pallasmaa (eds.), *Mind in Architecture: Neuroscience, Embodiment, and the Future of Design* (Cambridge, MA, 2015), 33-50: 40.
10 Guy Châtel, 'Stedenbouw (en architectuur) volgens artistieke principes', in: Christoph Grafe (ed.), *Radicale Gemeenplaatsen: Europese architectuur uit Vlaanderen: Architectuurboek Vlaanderen Vol. 10* (Antwerp, 2012), 258-267.
11 Johnson, 'The Embodied Meaning of Architecture', op. cit. (note 9), 41 ff.

# *The Belly of Naples and Displaced Meanings, City-as-Body and City-as-Theatre in Commentaries on the Old Town Risanamento*
## Deconstructing the Stereotype of the Picturesque

**Giuseppe Resta**

### Introduction

This article will discuss the formation of several stereotypical images associated with the picturesque nature of Southern Italy, by analysing the city of Naples. It interrogates two issues: first, how ethnographic interests created a strong bond between features of the people and the environment of Naples itself; second, how the use of literary tropes, especially 'city-as body' and 'city-as-theatre', influenced the reception of Naples abroad. The city has been endlessly described in guidebooks and travel accounts as the most important destination of the Grand Tour in Southern Italy. For this reason, we will limit our analysis to Neapolitan journalist Matilde Serao's writings on the subject, and selected pieces of literature written by foreign travellers before and after the *Risanamento* renewal period.

Naples also plays an important role in postcolonial studies on Southern Italy, primarily as the subject of many biased representations of the *Mezzogiorno*. For example, Franco Cassano repositioned the role of the South, and the Mediterranean region in general, as a self-aware agent of change.[1] As Ruth Glynn also pointed out in her critical analysis of Neapolitan cultural representations, the city has often been characterized as an uncivilized and barbaric place in need of corrections from civilized Northern Italy.[2] She also explains, in subsequent books and essays, about Walter Benjamin's concept of 'porosity' as alternative ways to embrace modernity. This link is also laid out in *Mediterranean Crossings* by Iain Chambers, who proposes that rather than resolve inequalities from a Western point of view, one should acknowledge the multiplicity of currents in cultural development – with the way we inhabit cities as one of them.[3] This is further explored by Fernand Braudel, Walter Benjamin, Henri Lefebvre's 'differential space' and many other Mediterranean voices.[4] Yet, the *meridionale* stereotype also surfaces in Benedetto Croce's work, whose understanding of the South as a historical space – instead of a geographical one – sets the stage for the newer paradigms of Italian historians like Giuseppe Galasso.[5] Massimo Cacciari also advocates for a 'geo-philosophy' of the Mediterranean, interpreting Naples' porosity in oppositional terms to Northern Europe,[6] while Glynn focuses on not creating construed dualism.[7] 'Southern Thought', in this sense, should both exist and develop independently of external forces. In that regard, John Dickie, in his review of stereotypes of Mezzogiorno from 1860-1990, argues it is difficult to discern who is 'us' and 'them' within the discourse, making the definition of a 'we' problematic.[8] Returning to the modernization issue, a southern urban theory has emerged with the argument that modernism, in certain regions, has 'never been a hegemonic culture'.[9] Hence, we must adopt an *ad hoc* theoretical framework of the very definition of progress and how we value it.

### Serao, Dickens, Benjamin and Sartre

As previously mentioned, early-modern travel culture produced a vast span of literature, which in turn contributed descriptions of local curiosities, peculiarities and so on eventually leading to typizations of both people and places in Naples.[10] Melissa Calaresu elaborates on a traveller's inability to escape the idea of a picturesque Naples, reinforcing a corresponding social determinism.[11] The urban setting then blends with images of street life, becoming an inseparable whole (Figs. 1-3).[12]

Fig. 1. Urban scene of the Neapolitan picturesque: street vendor. Photo by © Martina Russo, 2020.

Fig. 2. Urban scene of the Neapolitan picturesque: hanging clothes on the street, Pallonetto. Photo by © Martina Russo, 2020.

Fig. 3. Urban scene of the Neapolitan picturesque: religious statues and a wayside shrine in the public space, Montesanto station. Photo by © Fabiana Dicuonzo, 2018.

This article examines selected urban images reported before and after the dramatic renovations of the late nineteenth-century *Risanamento* period, with a focus on 'city-as-body' and 'city-as-theatre' tropes. We will also consider *Il Ventre di Napoli* (The Belly of Naples) by Matilde Serao, a Greek-born writer who was based in Naples – and, most importantly, published her text both right before the *Risanamento* and after its transformations. In the following two sections, we will see how Serao tackled contradictions of a constructed environment teeming with life via frequent references to the human body in order to capture spatial and social qualities of the city centre. In the last two sections of the article, we have connected excerpts from foreign travellers – again before and after the *Risanamento* – to pleasures (or sickness) of flesh and theatricality. These 'displaced meanings' parallel many descriptions by writers that travelled to Naples: Charles Dickens and the pantomime, Jean-Paul Sartre's delirium of flesh and rotten food, and Benjamin and the city-as-theatre. We argue that these pieces show how it is still possible to write about urban places, even in harsh terms like Sartre, while still deconstructing the stereotype of picturesqueness. In short, effort should be made to contextualize differences and understand the quality of urban space alongside the society that produces it.

For example, iconic thoroughfares, such as the Rettifilo and Toledo Street, can be thought of as scars upon the urban history of Naples. The first is a symbol of *Risanamento* in the late-nineteenth century, while the second divides the core of the city into two parts: the densely populated *Quartieri Spagnoli* to the west and the post-renovative Rione Carità to the east. Travellers who describe these environments frequently employ words that are related to the body and the organs. For instance, 'bowels' is a frequently used term to convey ideas of perceived spatiality when referring to the network of narrow alleyways in the old city.

Furthermore, Naples is seen as a sort of organism inhabited by bacteria that rots if left neglected. Under the lens of Jean-Paul Sartre's phenomenological ontology, this body is already sick.[13] Among the streets of the city, having recognized a perfect correspondence between the built environment and the men who inhabit it, the urban fabric is soft and wobbly. This impression of shapelessness comes from urban spaces expanding and contracting, like an abdomen full of primitive substances, which in turn is composed by the genes of an archaic civilization (Figs. 3-4).

**Matilde Serao and the Belly of Naples During the *Risanamento***

Journalist and novelist Matilde Serao, who was the founder (along with Edoardo Scarfoglio) of the Neapolitan daily newspaper *Il Mattino*, provided a personal and realistic description of Naples under the title *Il Ventre di Napoli* (The Belly of Naples). It was split into three different sections, each illustrating her conflicted feelings towards Neapolitan society. The first section of the book was written starting in 1884, when Serao was more critical and harsh towards the city. The last section was published in 1906, when Naples' degenerative immobility began to turn into an opportunity for possible redemption.

The climate at the end of the nineteenth century, to continue the metaphor, was literally feverish. A terrible cholera epidemic had put the issue of healthcare and traditional domestic spaces at the centre of public attention.[14] Consequently, urban renovations were being promoted by Mayor Nicola Amore: he deemed demolitions hygienically necessary to provide more natural light and ventilation throughout the city.[15] In fact, the reasons underlying relaxing the urban fabric were more complex, and involved the gentrification of façaded houses on the new and wide Rettifilo to maximize price. Furthermore, a wide and straight road piercing the belly of Naples allowed more efficient control of public places, especially to help combat popular uprisings.[16]

A few years earlier, between 1852 and 1870, prefect Georges-Eugène Haussmann had enforced the well-known 'Paris Renovation Plan', establishing an expropriation mechanism that led to mass demolitions of congested slums in the city centre. Rents instantly soared and caused an unprecedented displacement of the working class to the eastern periphery of the city.[17] While popular pressure increased on those in power in the French capital, including threats of rent strikes, similar operations of expanding corridors and landscaped squares were also not well-received in Naples. In its huge city centre, the cost of new houses was out of reach, and 'walking behind the screen [the Rettifilo]', Serao observed, such interventions did not affect the already existing 'ancient, damp, narrow, gloomy and dirty alleys'.[18] The Rettifilo, today called Corso Umberto I, is a straight 1-km boulevard, connecting the square in front of Naples Central Station with Giovanni Bovio square, before reaching the famous *Quartieri Spagnoli* by a steep street (Via Cardinale Guglielmo Sanfelice). It is a grand symbol of Nicola Amore's renovations . . . but also a great illusion. Serao describes it as an embalmed body – or rather, as a precarious scenography – with a thin layer concealing a completely different reality behind it. Furthermore, she overlapped the quality of the construction with that of an innkeeper she had met in the city, whom she described as having a 'yellowish face, livid lips, and black teeth'.[19]

It is therefore not surprising that urban planners used the word *sventramenti* (disembowelment) when addressing the corridors and boulevards that cut through crowded old towns at the end of the nineteenth century.[20] When Serao attempted to 're-place [the belly of Naples] within the connective tissue of the city-as-body, [she] metonymically grounds her proposal to reconstruct "rifare" the city and its people',[21] contrasting the façadism undertaken by politicians back then. Hence, Naples' belly contains food and waste, but also the potential to become a womb for rebirth.[22]

Keeping with the city-as-body trope, Serao reported that on the belly was a sort of laceration – cutting through flesh and exposing entrails teeming with life. From here, Serao warned that hidden viruses arose: beggars, thieves and fixers that would emerge from well-hidden alleys, striking and disappearing without leaving a trace, protected by their perfect knowledge of a porous space that bewildered anybody who happened to pass that way.[23]

**Serao, 20 Years Later: The Picturesque**

The second section of the book, written in 1903-1905 (and published in a new edition together with the previous section), employed a more detached look at the urban renewal phase twenty years after the approval of the *Risanamento* plan laid out by engineers Gaetano Bruno and Adolfo Giambarba.[24] Serao was increasingly more relaxed towards her city, though still disillusioned, she admitted in the preface. Social criticism turned into consideration of change. She believed that physical degeneration corresponded to moral degeneration, and rehabilitation could only be achieved after courageous decisions at the top. Honour could push Neapolitan society to seek redemption by placing illustrious men in the most important public offices. Financial straits, thereafter, would only be bad-faith arguments if investments were wisely allocated for the right causes.[25] For instance, a project at the time for Rione Della Bellezza – also known as Santa Lucia Nuova, an oceanside area with a view of the bay and Mount Vesuvius – was at the centre of public debate at the time. Interestingly, the urban renovations that were pitched seem to echo some of our contemporary marketing strategies; in particular, a picturesque name that endeavours to recall the values of Neapolitan landscape and tradition for the renovated property. This speculative venture included thirteen large blocks, one public garden and a 'Pompeian promenade' (a Greco-Roman-style portico). Nothing was 'more ugly, bulky, and heavy', Serao maintains.[26] She sensed how superficial the reference to tradition was when the project was *de facto* driven solely by the maximization of rental prices. Furthermore, the cost of a coastal home was expected to double. Injustice would be aggravated, Serao wrote, by the fact that the renovation would prevent Neapolitans and tourists from a full experience of the seascape.

Lastly, Toledo Street, also known as 'la gran via',[27] was a corridor connecting Piazza del Plebiscito to Piazza Dante through the belly of the city. Today, one can clearly recognize two distinct halves: the densely populated and porous *Quartieri Spagnoli* to the west, and the post-renovative *Rione Carità* with a loose urban fabric to the east.

Naples has long been associated with the picturesque, and its 'redemption' had to go beyond the physical transformation. It had to break century-old clichés. Charles Dickens visited Naples in February 1845: ten years before representing the divide of British society with the imagined industrial city of Coketown in his novel *Hard Times,* and forty years before the approval of the law on the *Risanamento*.[28] He saw the prerenovation Naples, and his first impression of the city was that of a funeral – a dead body shrouded with a red and golden cloth and carried in procession in an open bier. Death and life are well represented, he observed (Fig. 4). Arriving in the city, he felt all the inadequacy of 'lovers and hunters of the picturesque',[29] those who often idealize the precarious and degraded condition that is usually associated with the happy life of Neapolitans, as if it were inevitable. In Dickens's view, pantomime was the conventional sign for hunger, again a manifestation of bodily emptiness.[30] While the English writer was more impressed by the rural landscape of Naples, Serao associated the picturesque city centre's 'belly' with the appropriation of public space by grocers. Shopkeepers or street vendors had arranged the city spaces in multiple ways, forming a spatial 'seizure', in order to express their public persona.[31] Looking at the streetscape, Serao asked herself: '[If] the shops are there but everything is for sale on the street; sidewalks have disappeared, who has ever seen them?'.[32]

'Touristization' of Neapolitan folklore had already commenced at the beginning of the nineteenth century, as Stendhal noted on one of his stays. He visited Naples and other major cities with an idealized vision, right before

Fig. 4. Fontanelle cemetery, a charnel house located in a cave under the Sanità neighbourhood where people developed a spontaneous cult of devotion to skulls. Photo by © Fabiana Dicuonzo, 2018.

the Golden Age of travel in the peninsula (1815-1830).[33] But he was still more interested in people's relation with the constructed environment, as Sartre was, rather than ruins and museums. When Stendhal stepped outside the door of Palazzo Degli Studi where he was based, he walked onto Toledo Street, *'un des grands buts de mon voyage, la rue plus peuplée et la plus gaie de l'univers'*,[34] full of English tourists as it was becoming one of the main destinations of the Grand Tour. Toledo is perhaps the deepest cut in the belly of Naples, a mark that shows all the *strata* of Neapolitan souls, 'hearth of hearts: via Toledo! The stream of humankind'.[35]

**Jean-Paul Sartre's Naples: A Delirium of Flesh and Rotten Food**

Additionally, falsehood and deception were at the centre of Sartre's reportage *Nourritures* (Nourishments),[36] written and published two years after his stay in post-renovation Naples in 1936. During his stay, he discovered 'love's vile relationship to Food. Not right away. Naples doesn't show itself at first. It's a town which is ashamed of itself',[37] leading to a sort of hallucinatory drift within the narrative voice. It is a simple ballad in which Naples' teeming streets trigger his mental and physical alteration:[38]

> *At the bottom of a hole in the wall, there was a shape in a bed. It was a young woman, a sick woman. She was suffering; she turned her head toward the street – her throat made a tender spot above the sheets. I stopped; I looked at her for a long time; I would have liked to run my hands over her skinny neck – I shook myself and strode rapidly away. But it was too late; I was trapped. I no longer saw a thing but flesh: wretched flowers of flesh waving in blue darkness; flesh to palpate, suck, and eat; wet flesh soaked with sweat, urine, milk.*[39]

The dialectic between the inhabitants and the places they lived in, in the eyes of the Parisian philosopher, took place primarily through food, as a mirror of Naples' external and ephemeral appearance. Food in grocery shops is bright and splendid, and pastry shops look 'like a jewelry store',[40] showing cakes of cruel perfection, coloured and polished like jewels behind the windows. Then, around the corner of the *Caflisch* pastry shop in a narrow street, he sees a slice of watermelon on the ground – open and spotted with mud. It was 'buzzing with flies like rotting flesh and bleeding underneath the dying rays of the sun. A child on crutches came up to this rotten meat, took it in his hands, and began to eat it with gusto.'[41] This contradiction between the shiny surface of jewel-like cakes and rotten foods that can be found around the corner frequently parallels with Serao's aforementioned 'screen', but also with the fleeting beauty of the body. Both works concern themselves with the duplicity of Naples, and narrativize primitivism and widespread precariousness emerging from the 'masses of filthy, crumbling, miserable houses of all sizes, stained with all the stigmata of poverty and vice'.[42] Many commentators see within this fluid identity the mechanism of indeterminacy that constitutes a sort of feminine space – a mother-city according to Natalia Rita Giannini's dissertation[43] – in which emptiness, or nothingness, is not seen relative to the phallus of subjectivity. Rather, it is a womb that nourishes and bestows life-giving power on the subject. Fluidity is then the base of its grotesque aesthetic, being 'a city that asserts fragmentation and segmentation instead of completeness and linearity'[44] in a precarious relationship between mother and child.

### Benjamin and the City-as-Theatre

That same fluidity transforms daily practices into acts of spatial appropriation, usually represented in the form of a pseudo-musical in which alleyways and public squares are flooded with singers and dancers. In analysing the musical corporeality of Naples, Giuliana Bruno notes that 'the musicality and street life of the city ultimately have been transformed into an internationally constructed folklore'.[45] John Turturro's documentary *Passione* (2010) offers a perfect explanation of this *topos*, with the city-as-theatre and masses of bodies living their melodramatic lives. It is a densely populated film, with artistic narcissism 'performed on traffic island and *terrazzi*, in bistros and at the bus stops, on beaches and in beds',[46] while architectural elements of the public space are used as makeshift stages. The comparison of syncopated body movements with urban features such as stairs, intersections and balconies is made evident by Walter Benjamin and Asja Lacis in Naples in 1924, three years before the initiation of his *Passagenwerk* project. He introduced the idea of porosity associated with the built environment:

> *. . . as porous as this stone is the architecture. Building and action interpenetrate in the courtyards, arcades, and stairways. In everything, they preserve the scope to become a theatre of new, unforeseen constellations. The stamp of the definitive is avoided. No situation appears intended forever, no figure asserts its 'thus and not otherwise'.*[47]

On this kind of large-scale stage, the more that events are spurred on by chaos, the more separations between public and private will become blurred. Theatrical components are a direct expression of Neapolitans' passion for improvisation, which temporarily reconfigures streets, staircases, roofs, entryways and more as improvised scenes on the stage of everyday life. Private life is 'fragmented, porous and discontinuous. What distinguishes Naples from other large cities is something it has in common with the African *kraal*; each private attitude or act is permeated by streams of communal life.'[48] The aforementioned 'nourishing emptiness' is here crystallized into 'porosity', which expresses the fraction of voids over the total volume. If the metaphor is applicable in architecture, porosity then represents the ability of the urban fabric to be permeated by public space and activate urbanity.[49] Streets penetrate domestic spaces, and vice versa. Porosity is evident on the iconic Palazzo Dello Spagnolo (Fig. 5), in the Sanità neighbourhood, as permeable as volcanic slag from Vesuvius. Additionally, complex systems of staircases overlap the inner façades of the courtyards, creating diaphanous thresholds on multiple levels in Palazzo Trabucco, Palazzo Venezia, Palazzo Sanfelice (Fig. 6) and Palazzo di Majo. Benjamin's text, though with a different set of tropes and metaphors, also

Fig. 5. Courtyard of Palazzo Dello Spagnolo.

Fig. 6. Courtyard of Palazzo Sanfelice.
Photos by © Fabiana Dicuonzo, 2018.

pointed towards the dark and shapeless form of the old town, where modernity has not penetrated.[50] Furthermore, Glynn notes that Benjamin's celebration of such spatial practices challenged those established categories, such as the private and the public distinction, posing itself as an ideal counterpart to Northern Europe.[51]

**Conclusions**

Serao's texts provided a passionate account of a pulsating Naples, then-struggling with its density. Organic growth leads to a porous constructed environment, in which public spaces are at times connected, or conversely trapped like air pockets. As porosity in geology is a product of its own formation, Naples likewise grew (and grows) with overlapping layers and vistas – creating an iridescent vision that is difficult to summarize with mere physical description. The Naples that Serao recounted is still a malleable rock, then-sedimenting with sudden, painful and even catastrophic events, as if a wounded body. In the following 150 years, the belly of Naples would mineralize, while still living with the cliché of the picturesque. Over time, the pores solidify, and today what we see is the rough surface of a rock with all of the dramatic vital pulsations of its past still visible.

We have seen previous writings provide ground for an identification of the body of people with that of the city. On the other end, environmental determinism and oversimplification (such as tourists in search of curiosities) contributes to establishing stereotypical images, which, in turn, may push the tourism industry to respond to that demand and offer a staged picturesqueness of the city. Writing about cities like Naples poses many difficulties in discerning similarities and differences with other European cities. Rhetoric can overlap authenticity, and generalization devalues the richness of details. Following the analysis in this text, we propose to embrace fragmentation, and thereby renounce the idea of a comprehensive synthesis of the city.

1 See his idea of *pensiero meridiano* (southern thought) in Franco Cassano, *Il pensiero meridiano* (Roma-Bari, 1996) and Franco Cassano, *Tre modi di vedere il Sud* (Bologna, 2009). *Il pensiero meridiano* is available in an English edition published by Fordham University Press in 2012.

2 Ruth Glynn, 'Porosity and Its Discontents: Approaching Naples in Critical Theory', *Cultural Critique* 107 (2020), 63-98.

3 Iain Chambers, *Mediterranean Crossings: The Politics of an Interrupted Modernity* (Durham, NC, 2008).

4 Henri Lefebvre, *The Production of Space*, translated by Donald Nicholson-Smith (Oxford and Cambridge, 1991).

5 Giuseppe Galasso, *L'altra Europa: Per un'antropologia storica del Mezzogiorno d'Italia* (Milan, 1982).

6 Massimo Cacciari, 'Non potete massacrarmi Napoli!', in: Claudio Velardi (ed.), *La città porosa: Conversazioni su Napoli* (Naples, 1992), 157-190.

7 Glynn, 'Porosity and Its Discontents', op. cit. (note 2).

8 John Dickie, *Darkest Italy: The Nation and Stereotypes of the Mezzogiorno, 1860-1900* (New York, 1999).

9 Lila Leontidou, 'Alternatives to Modernism in (Southern) Urban Theory: Exploring in-between Spaces', *International Journal of Urban and Regional Research* 20/2 (1996), 180.

10 On the common ground shared by tourism and anthropology, see: Dennison Nash and Valene L. Smith, 'Anthropology and Tourism', *Annals of Tourism Research* 18/1 (1991), 12-25; and Tom Selwyn, 'Anthropology and Tourism', *Tourism Management* 11/1 (1990), 68-69.

11 Melissa Calaresu, 'From the Street to Stereotype: Urban Space, Travel and the Picturesque in Late Eighteenth-Century Naples', *Italian Studies* 62/2 (2007), 189-203.

12 Ibid.

13 Jean-Paul Sartre, *Spaesamento: Napoli E Capri* (Naples, 2000). Originally published in *Œuvres romanesques* in 1982 under the title 'Dépaysement'.

14 Giuseppe Sanarelli, *Il colera: epidemiologia, patologia, batteriologia, terapia e profilassi* (Milan, 1931).

15 Elena Manzo, 'Il "Risanamento" di Napoli. Dal progetto urbano alla scala architettonica', *Atti e Rassegna Tecnica della Società degli Ingegneri e degli Architetti in Torino* 72/1 (2018), 113-122.

16 Daniela Lepore, 'Il Centro Storico Di Napoli: Vecchi Propositi E Nuovi Progetti', *Meridiana* 5 (1989), 129-142.

17 Ann-Louise Shapiro, 'Housing Reform in Paris: Social Space and Social Control', *French Historical Studies* 12/4 (1982), 486-507.
18 Author's translation of 'camminando dietro il paravento' and 'vicoli antichi, umidi, alti, tetri e sporchi', in: Matilde Serao, *Il Ventre Di Napoli: Venti Anni Fa* (Naples, 1906), 101-102.
19 Author's translation of 'viso giallastro, sulle sue labbra violette, nei suoi denti neri', in: ibid., 109.
20 Leonardo Benevolo, *The Origins of Modern Town Planning*, translated by Judith Landry (London, 1967).
21 Darby Tench, 'Gutting the Belly of Naples: Metaphor, Metonymy and the Auscultatory Imperative in Serao's City of "Pietà"', *Annali d'Italianistica* 7 (1989), 288-289.
22 Ibid.
23 Serao, *Il Ventre Di Napoli*, op. cit. (note 18).
24 Manzo, 'Il "Risanamento" di Napoli', op. cit. (note 15).
25 Serao, *Il Ventre Di Napoli*, op. cit. (note 18).
26 Author's translation of 'Nulla di più brutto, di più goffo, di più pesante', in: Serao, *Il Ventre Di Napoli*, op. cit. (note 18), 149.
27 Ibid., 156.
28 Maria Gabriella Caponi-Doherty, 'Charles Dickens and the Italian Risorgimento', *Dickens Quarterly* 13/3 (1996), 151-163.
29 Charles Dickens, *Pictures from Italy* (London, 1846), 240.
30 Ibid.
31 Serao, *Il Ventre Di Napoli*, op. cit. (note 18), 67.
32 Author's translation of 'vi sono le botteghe ma tutto si vende nella via; i marciapiedi sono scomparsi, chi li ha mai visti?', in: ibid., 69.
33 Rosemary Sweet, Gerrit Verhoeven and Sarah Goldsmith (eds.), *Beyond the Grand Tour: Northern Metropolises and Early Modern Travel Behaviour* (London, 2017).
34 Stendhal, *Rome, Naples Et Florence* (Paris, 1817), 61. Translated by Richard Coe as 'one of the principal goals of all my journey, the busiest, most joyous thoroughfare in the entire universe', in: Stendhal, *Rome, Naples and Florence*, translated by Richard N. Coe (London, 1959), 350.
35 Author's translation of 'cuore dei cuori: Via Toledo! Il torrente dell'umanità', in: Serao, *Il Ventre Di Napoli*, op. cit. (note 18), 159.
36 Fragment of a story published for the first time as 'Nourritures', in: *Verve*,

November 15, 1938. In Italy, it was published with the title 'I vicoli di Napoli' (The alleys of Naples) in *Lotta Continua*, April 17, 1980, 20. Then it was incorporated in Sartre, *Spaesamento*, op. cit. (note 13).

37 Michel Rybalka and Michel Contat (eds.), *The Writings of Jean-Paul Sartre*, vol. 2, Studies in Phenomenology & Existential Philosophy (Evanston, 1974), 60.

38 Tobias Haberkorn, 'Se Sentir Napolitain: Voir, Vivre, Écrire La Ville Avec Goethe, Sartre, Malaparte Et Saviano', *Eurostudia* 8/1-2 (2012), 149-169.

39 Rybalka and Contat, *The Writings of Jean-Paul Sartre*, op. cit. (note 37), 62.

40 Ibid., 61.

41 Ibid.

42 Author's translation of 'masse di case lerce, cadenti, miserabili, di tutte le misure, macchiate di tutte le stigmate della povertà e del vizio', in: Serao, *Il Ventre Di Napoli*, op. cit. (note 18), 93.

43 Natalia Rita Giannini, *Naples: The Mother City* (Boca Raton, 2003).

44 Ibid., 6.

45 Giuliana Bruno, *Atlas of Emotion* (London, 2002), §11.

46 Irwin Chusid, 'John Turturro's Passione Stays True to the Music', *Filmcomment* (September/October 2011), 16.

47 Walter Benjamin, *Reflections: Essays, Aphorisms, Autobiographical Writings* (New York, 1986), 165-166.

48 Ibid., 171.

49 The success of this acceptance is probably due to Steven Holl formulating the shift from typological towards topological conception in: Steven Holl, *Parallax* (New York, 2000).

50 Daniele Dottorini, 'Rileggere Benjamin: la forma della città, la doppia immagine della modernità', *Cahiers d'études romanes* 19 (2008), 153-166.

51 Glynn, 'Porosity and Its Discontents', op. cit. (note 2).

# *Appropriation and Gendered Spaces*
# A Discussion on Elena Ferrante's Neapolitan Novels

**Sernaz Arslan**

Within the framework of Gillian Rose and Doreen Massey's theoretical conceptualizations regarding space, this article aims to discuss appropriation of urban space from a gendered perspective as presented through the Neapolitan novels by Elena Ferrante. Ferrante's tetralogy not only portrays the personal transformation of the main characters Lenú and Lila, but also their practices of urban appropriation, their relationship with the neighbourhood they live in, and the transformation of Naples as a socially constructed space itself.

In recent years, Elena Ferrante's Neapolitan novels have received worldwide popular and critical attention. Tackling issues such as gender, motherhood, marriage, female friendship, poverty and post-Second World War politics, Ferrante's work reaches across different cultures and societies. It also constitutes a rich and substantial framework for multidisciplinary academic discussions and analyses. Indeed, the four volumes provide a fertile ground to discuss the relationship between place and gender throughout the second half of twentieth-century Naples. Translated and published in English between 2012 and 2015, the series has been characterized as a female *bildungsroman* that begins in 1950s Naples. It follows the lives of two protagonists, Elena (Lenù) Greco and Raffaella (Lila) Cerullo, from childhood to old age, as they struggle to find their ways amid the violence and poverty driven post-Second World War Naples. While navigating the sharp social and economic divides of the city, the two characters try to figure out what they want to become by challenging the dominant gender roles and power relations embedded in the society. This article aims to discuss appropriation of urban space from a gendered perspective as presented through the novels. To do so, it begins with a brief contextualization of space and appropriation within the framework of feminist geography.

**Situating Space, Gender and Appropriation**

Over the last few decades, scholars from different disciplines have been trying to understand how environments, landscapes, architectural surroundings, places and spaces have influenced the nature and scope of political power, cultural production, social experience and construction of identities.[1] A significant number of scholars has contributed to the definition of place, space and the differences between these concepts. According to Dolores Hayden, place is one of the trickiest words in English. It indicates homestead, location and position in social hierarchy.[2] Yi-Fu Tuan, Edward Relph and Tim Creswell, among others, have associated the concept of place with human experience, action, intention and attachment.[3] Space, on the other hand, has been perceived as something more abstract, without any substantial meaning. Tuan described space as a location that has no social connections.[4] Furthermore, in the early 1980s, humanities and social sciences approached the concept of space from a different angle. Inspired by the work of Michel Foucault and Henri Lefebvre, scholars like David Harvey and Edward Soja argued that space was not a static, abstract location without any social connections, emotions and meaning. It was dynamic, constructed and contested. As asserted by Foucault, 'space is fundamental in any exercise of power'.[5] Space is where issues of class, sexuality, gender and race are located, shaped and fought out.

Feminist scholars played a pioneering role in this spatial turn. In the early 1970s feminist geographers started to underline both the neglect of women and the existing stereotypes concerning gender in human geography. The urban space became not only a crucial scale through which gender is experienced and constituted, but also a conceptual framework within which the socioeconomic aspects of human life could be analysed.[6] Over the years the agendas of feminist urban studies have been enriched with the perspective of socialist feminism, identity politics, empathy, and politics of recognition and redistribution. As Leslie Kern asserts: 'Feminist urban studies mean tackling a complex web of power relations.'[7] Feminist urban studies asks a set of questions concerning the societal relations in the city/urban space; looking at them through the lens of gender, sexuality, race, class, accessibility; acknowledging and discussing various urban experiences while keeping intersectionality intact.[8]

By proposing questions about how spaces are experienced differently by various actors, feminist geographers began to challenge the existing assumptions about the place of women and men in societies, built environments and the relationships within which they live and work. Their focus on the presence and absence of different groups in urban spaces brought issues of participation and non-participation into the framework. However, their contribution has been more than bringing issues of gender and factors like age, class and ethnicity into the field of urban studies. While rethinking gender and its relationship to space, feminist geographers also revisited the key concept of space. It is thus not possible to talk about a singular, concrete and stable definition of space. As argued by Liz Bondi and Joyce Davidson, feminist geography enabled new and interconnected ways of thinking about space and gender.[9]

It can be argued that there are two main approaches towards space and gender. The first, based on Doreen Massey's analysis, conceptualizes space and gender as interrelated, mutually constitutive processes. Like Lefebvre, Massey also perceives space as a social construct. It is based on the dynamic interplay between values and the continuous production and reproduction of meanings. She states that defining space as a notion producing shared experiences leaves us unable to see how differences in gender, age and class, along with other forms of social differentiation, shape individuals' lives.[10] Such a conceptualization of space fails to acknowledge how social relations shape the urban space. Not all individuals experience urban space in the same way, due to the societal power relations embedded in it. Therefore, space cannot be described as a notion creating shared experiences and providing similar opportunities and possibilities for all. There are numerous examples in the literature illustrating this argument based on the theory of space and gender as mutually constructed.[11]

The second influential approach concerning space in feminist geography literature has its origins in Gillian Rose's controversial description of 'paradoxical space'. Rose examines the relationship between space and gender within the framework of contradictions that represents women's everyday experiences. According to her, paradoxical space 'is a space imagined in order to articulate a troubled relation to the hegemonic discourses of masculinism'.[12] In other words, through the paradoxical space it is possible to challenge and reverse the dominant practices and conceptualizations of gender. For Rose, the built environment surrounding us is a product of the male/masculine imagination. This creates an obstacle for women to claim rights and/or control over space. To overcome this obstacle, women should insist on the possibility of resistance and change. Paradoxical space has the potential to replace the dominant, hegemonic, masculinist space and make a more equal, free space possible.[13]

These conceptualizations of space pave the way for a gendered discussion of appropriation. Like the term space, appropriation does not have a single definition as well. According to Lefebvre, appropriation refers to people's acts when they exert their right to the city and urban places as spaces of encounter.[14] As they appropriate the city space, inhabitants should be able to use the city for themselves and give a novel shape to the urban environment. In that sense, appropriation is an act of reorientation.[15] As Mark Purcell indicates, Lefebvre's conceptualization of appropriation is based on urban inhabitants owning the city.[16] But he does not discuss ownership within the framework of property rights; according to him 'the city belongs to those who inhabit it'.[17] The issue of ownership is also central to Perla Korosec-Serfaty's definition of appropriation. She defines appropriation as a way of 'possessing and managing space, irrespective of its legal ownership, for its everyday use or as a means of identification'.[18] Some scholars explain appropriation as a process by which people are constantly reclaiming urban spaces,[19] or as a mechanism that leads to the development of place attachment and place identity.[20] It is also discussed as an interactive process through which individuals transform their physical environment into a meaningful place while being transformed themselves in turn.[21]

Regardless of how the term is defined, the way women and men appropriate urban spaces is different. As demonstrated by Massey's theory of space, their experiences of urban spaces differ due to norms and expectations based on perceptions of gender. Female gender identity shapes how women move through the city, how and to what extent they participate in urban public life, what choices are available to them. In fact, in cities women seem to have choices that would not be available to them in small, rural towns, such as developing new networks, having opportunities for work and education, going after non-traditional careers, avoiding marriage and motherhood, and participating in arts, culture, social and political events.[22] However, gendered discourses constitute a constant reminder that women should limit their freedom to walk, work, have fun and exist in the urban space. Their appropriation practices remain rather planned for certain urban spaces, for certain timeframes. It is the paradoxical space that allows for spontaneous, participative, flexible and meaningful appropriation.

Ferrante's Neapolitan novels not only portray the personal transformation of the main characters Lenú and Lila, but also their practices of urban appropriation and their relationship with the neighbourhood they live in, along with the transformation of Naples as a socially constructed space itself.

**Appropriation in Ferrante's Naples and the Neighbourhood**

As mentioned already, Naples is the setting of Ferrante's story. Lenú and Lila grow up in a miserable neighbourhood, named *rione*, that is characterized by poverty, violence, the Camorra and dominant patriarchal gender norms. Even though Ferrante describes the neighbourhood in detail, she does not reveal its name. She does, however, name each street and square when the characters leave the neighbourhood they lived in and move into other parts of the city, as if she would like to attribute a certain degree of universality to the neighbourhood. Without disregarding the uniqueness of Naples and the *rione*, it can be argued that Ferrante presents it as an archetype for a space dominated by poverty, violence and patriarchal power relations.

Ferrante's representation of Naples, in particular the neighbourhood, constructs a space dominated by male imagery and codes of masculinity. Women's presence and participation in urban spaces are limited and controlled by the male members of their family. Being mainly confined to the private sphere of their homes, women are present in the courtyard in front of their buildings, which become an extension of their apartments. Grocery shopping appears to be the major spatial experience of women in the neighbourhood, especially for married women and mothers. Such a representation of the *rione* is a manifestation of Massey's conceptualization of space. Ferrante's female characters' opportunities and possibilities of urban appropriation are dictated by the patriarchal power relations embedded in the Neapolitan society.

Starting from the first book of the series, *My Brilliant Friend* (2011), Lenú and Lila try to escape the limitations, both intellectual and spatial, imposed on them by their neighbourhood. In that sense, the neighbourhood presents a paradigm that resists change from one generation to the next. Their desire to escape this dominant paradigm is reflected in the girls' obsession with generating wealth, excelling in reading and writing, getting rid of their dialect and mastering Italian. The tunnel and how it's appropriated by Lenú and Lila also illustrate their desire to escape the limitations associated with the neighbourhood. The main road out of the neighbourhood leads to a dark, infamous tunnel with three entrances. Through that tunnel it is possible to reach wealthier parts of Naples and the sea. Lenú and Lila's first attempt to leave the neighbourhood is by walking through that tunnel to go and see the sea. But the two girls did not reach their goal that day: Lila got scared and they turned back. When they did manage to go through the tunnel and visit other parts of the city, namely Via Chiaia, they were astonished. 'It was like crossing a border,' narrates Lenú, 'I remember a dense crowd and a sort of humiliating difference. I looked not at the boys but at the girls, the women: they were absolutely different from us. They seemed to have breathed another air, to have eaten other food, to have dressed on some other planet, to have learned to walk on wisps of air.'[23] There were women having drinks and laughing in cafés, girls walking alone by themselves in pretty dresses, couples walking down the street hand in hand. Lenú, who is not allowed to leave the neighbourhood without being chaperoned by her male friends, is faced with a strwong sense of non-belonging:

Source: Juniper Books.

> *They didn't see any of the five of us. We were not perceptible. Or not interesting. And in fact, if at times their gaze fell on us, they immediately turned in another direction, as if irritated. They looked only at each other. Of this we were all aware. No one mentioned it, but we understood that Rino and Pasquale, who were older, found on those streets only confirmation of things they already knew, and this put them in a bad mood, made them sullen, resentful at the certainty of being out of place, while we girls discovered it only at that moment and with ambiguous sentiments.*[24]

It can be argued that the feeling of being out of place experienced by the girls is different compared to how it is experienced by Rino and Pasquale. The boys have been out of the *rione* before. They have already faced urban spaces they could not afford to participate in. Accordingly, their sense of non-belonging is rather class-based. However, for the girls it's a completely new urban space, which they are not even able to appropriate without the company of a male figure. They were astonished and felt out of place when they saw the women and girls walking down the streets on their own, not hindered by the patriarchal gender norms.

The first two books of the series, *My Brilliant Friend* (2011) and *The Story of a New Name* (2012), can be regarded as Lenú and Lila's struggle to find a way to challenge their built environment, the space they live in. Being able to go through the tunnel, to move beyond the limits of the neighbourhood, indicates the possibility of different forms of appropriation in Neapolitan urban space that is composed by diverse social layers. In that sense, Piazza dei Martiri is depicted as a gateway to this diversity. The square is in the affluent Chiaia district, where Lenú and Lila felt like being in an alien world, crossing an invisible border. The square symbolizes a change with respect to the protagonists' relationship with the space. According to Lefebvre, urban appropriation should not be dispersed to the periphery of a city. It should also cover the right to use of the centre. Their presence, involvement, actions and decision in the Piazza dei Martiri can be considered as the beginning of the transformation they engage in. In the Piazza, Lenú and Lila challenged not only the spatial boundaries that were imposed on them, but also the patriarchal power relations embedded in the society. It is in the Piazza that Lenú decides to go to Pisa for higher education; Lila continues to have an extramarital affair and later decides to leave both the neighbourhood and her husband.

Recalling Rose's theory of space, the *rione* is a metaphor for paradoxical space. Rose presents paradoxical space as a space where power, knowledge and identity are renegotiated and redefined.[25] She focuses on how women experience confinement in a space in their everyday lives. For her the key point is that women are located in both public and private space, in the centre and the margin. They are both insiders and outsiders. In her work, Rose discusses the paradoxes of occupying these spaces and underlines how challenging they can be: 'The simultaneous occupation of centre and margin can critique the authority of masculinism . . . help[ing] some feminists to think about both recognizing differences between women and continuing to struggle for change as women.'[26] As women start to exert more agency and to challenge existing masculinist discourses and hegemonic identities, space becomes paradoxical space, which is dynamic, fluid, heterogenous and subjective.

In the third and fourth book of the series, *Those Who Leave and Those Who Stay* (2013) and *The Story of the Lost Child* (2014), Lenú and Lila return to the neighbourhood equipped with different resources, like education, employment and wealth. Lila, who was still married but living with another man in the neighbourhood 'had a very new job, she earned a lot of money, she acted in absolute freedom and according to schemes that were indecipherable'.[27] Lenú, on the other hand, acknowledged that she had a sort of double identity:

*The result was that on Via Tasso and throughout Italy I felt like a woman with a small reputation, whereas in Naples, especially in the neighbourhood, I lost my refinement, no one knew anything about my second book, if injustices enraged me, I moved into dialect and the coarsest insults.*[28]

'And in fact, I felt like an external observer, with inadequate information',[29] narrates Lenú in the aftermath of her return to the neighbourhood where she was struggling to assert herself.

Once representing getting away from the neighbourhood, the tunnel this time depicts their return. 'From Via Tasso the old neighbourhood was a dim, distant rockpile, indistinguishable urban debris at the foot of Vesuvius,' narrates Lenú, 'I wanted it to stay that way: I was another person now, I would make sure that it did not recapture me.'[30] Thinking about appropriation is also thinking about change and transformation. While the heroines make their own choices and challenge the existing gendered power relations and structures, they also transform the neighbourhood as a space. Upon her return, Lenú was 'immediately seized by a yearning to regain possession of the neighborhood'.[31] Both she and Lila start to make a spatial claim in the Lefebvrian sense and exert strong agency in terms of their appropriation. While Lenú challenges the gendered power relations embedded in the neighbourhood by publishing a journal article about the Solara Brothers, who were members of the Camorra, Lila does it by means of her newly established business. Lila's significant claim concerning the neighbourhood is reflected in the following quotation:

*It was no different on the streets of the neighbourhood. Going shopping with her never ceased to amaze me: she had become an authority. She was constantly stopped, people drew her aside with a respectful familiarity, they whispered something to her, and she listened, without reacting. Did they treat her like that because of the success she had had*

> *with her new business? Because she gave off the sense of someone who could do anything?*[32]

Ferrante's *rione* becomes a paradoxical space; a space of resistance and transformation that enables a more equal, spontaneous appropriation.

As stated by Sara Santos Cruz, appropriation is about writing personal stories in urban places and creating narratives throughout the city.[33] The Neapolitan novels tell the story of two women who struggle to find new ways to write their own stories and prove that it is possible to create a new neighbourhood. The novels depict different stages in their lives and different attempts to appropriate the urban spaces in which they find themselves: 'Lila the shoemaker, Lila who imitated Kennedy's wife, Lila the artist and designer, Lila the worker, Lila the programmer, Lila always in the same place and always out of place',[34] and Lenú, who travelled places to become herself and managed to do it by confronting boundaries imposed on her. Through the urban experiences of her female characters Ferrante shows how urban space and gender are intertwined and mutually influential, both for her female and male characters. Moreover, as mentioned above, space is where issues of class, sexuality, gender and race are located, shaped and fought out.

1 Kathryne Beebe, Angela Davis and Kathryn Gleadle, 'Introduction: Space, Place and Gendered Identities: Feminist History and the Spatial Turn', *Women's History Review* 21/4 (2012), 523-532.

2 Dolores Hayden, *The Power of Place: Urban Landscapes as Public History* (Boston, 1997), 15.

3 Yi-Fu Tuan, *Space and Place: The Perspective of Experience* (Minnesota, 1977); Edward Relph, *Place and Placelessness* (London, 1976); Tim Creswell, *Place: A Short Introduction* (Malden, 2004).

4 Tuan, *Space and Place*, op. cit. (note 3), 6.
5 Michel Foucault, *The Foucault Reader* (New York, 1984), 252.
6 Linda McDowell, 'Towards an Understanding of the Gender Division of Urban Space', *Environment and Planning D: Society and Space* 1/1 (1983), 59-72.
7 Leslie Kern, *Feminist City: Claiming Space in a Man-made World* (London, 2020), 47.
8 The term intersectionality was first used by Kimberlé Crenshaw in the late 1980s. It was mainly developed to indicate that race and gender are not mutually exclusive and cannot be analysed separately. Intersectionality has always been an important part of feminist geography. The intersections between gender, sexuality, ethnicity, age, class, religion, ability and nationality are part of feminist geographers' research. Gill Valentine, Audrey Kobayashi, Linda Peake, Leslie McCall and Ann Hancock, among others, have contributed to the development of intersectionality in feminist geography literature. Doreen Massey's arguments regarding space imply that places and space do not only entail a variety of intersectional relations, but they also create and shape these intersectional relations.
9 Liz Bondi and Joyce Davidson, 'Situating Gender', in: Lise Nelson and Joni Seager (eds.), *A Companion to Feminist Geography* (New Jersey, 2005), 15-31.
10 Doreen Massey, 'Politics and Space/Time', *New Left Review* 196 (1992), 65.
11 For some examples, please see: Koskela Hille, '"Gendered Exclusions": Women's Fear of Violence and Changing Relations to Space', *Geografiska Annaler: Series B, Human Geography* 81/2 (1999), 111-124; Gill Valentine, 'The Geography of Women's Fear', *Area* 21/4 (1989), 385-390; Gerda R. Wekerle, 'Women's Rights to the City: Gendered Spaces of a Pluralistic Citizenship', in: Engin F. Isin (ed.), *Democracy, Citizenship, and the Global City* (London, 2000), 203-217.
12 Gillian Rose, *Feminism & Geography: The Limits of Geographical Knowledge* (Minnesota, 1993), 159.
13 Ibid., 155.
14 Henri Lefebvre, *Writings on Cities* (Cambridge, 1996), 174.
15 Henri Lefebvre, *The Urban Revolution* (Minnesota, 2003), 1.
16 Mark Purcell, 'Possible Worlds: Henri Lefebvre and the Right to the City', *Journal of Urban Affairs* 36/1 (2014), 141-154.
17 Ibid., 149.
18 Perla Korosec-Serfaty, 'The Home from Attic to Cellar', *Journal of Environmental Psychology* 4/4 (1985), 303-321.
19 Frank O. Ostermann and Sabine Timpf, 'Use and Appropriation of Space in Urban Public Parks: GIS Methods in Social Geography', *Geographica Helvetica* 64/1 (2009), 30-36.

20 Harold M. Proshansky, 'The Appropriation and Misappropriation of Space', in: *Appropriation of Space: Proceedings of the Strasbourg Conference* (Louvain-la-Neuve, 1976), 31-45.
21 Roberta M. Feldman and Susan Stall, 'The Politics of Space Appropriation', in: Irwin Altman and Arza Churchman (eds.), *Women and the Environment* (Boston, 1994), 167-199.
22 Kern, *Feminist City*, op. cit. (note 7), 159.
23 Elena Ferrante, *My Brilliant Friend* (London, 2012), 192.
24 Ibid., 193.
25 Rose, *Feminism & Geography*, op. cit. (note 12), 140.
26 Ibid., 152-153.
27 Elena Ferrante, *Those Who Leave and Those Who Stay* (London, 2014), 358.
28 Ibid., 370.
29 Ibid., 369.
30 Elena Ferrante, *The Story of the Lost Child* (London, 2020), 116.
31 Ibid., 261.
32 Ibid., 205.
33 Sara Santos Cruz, 'Appropriation as Transformative, Manipulative and Affective', keynote speech at online mini conference 'Meaningfulness, Appropriation and Integration of/in City Narratives' by COST Action 18126 Working Group 2, 17 November 2020.
34 Ferrante, *The Story of the Lost Child*, op. cit. (note 30), 477.

# *Narratives of Appropriation* Abandoned Spaces, Entangled Stories and Profound Urban Transformations

**Dalia Milián Bernal**

> *It is not just saying, 'I want to occupy a space', rather, it is 'I want to create concrete examples of the kind of country I want to live in' . . . that is the power of urban activation and community activation and all that is related with manifesting the dreams and the imagination physically.*
> *Sofía Unanue, personal communication, 21 February 2018*

Sofía's statement is a powerful one and can only be understood when contextualized. The day I interviewed her, she was talking to me from her home in the city of San Juan in Puerto Rico. It had only been a couple of months after Maria – a Category 5 hurricane – struck the island in September 2017, ploughing its way through the fields, destroying an already fragile urban infrastructure, disconnecting towns from any form of communication – not to mention killing thousands of people and leaving many others without home or shelter.[1]

As claimed elsewhere, the hurricane is only partly at fault for the devastation, because Puerto Rico's social, economic and political systems were already in precarious conditions before the passing of Maria.[2] For years, the island had been subjected to land grabbing and unregulated resource extraction and plunged into a financial crisis. In 2016, a fiscal board was appointed to oversee and manage the economic crisis. Known as La Junta, the board put in place harsh austerity measures that further impoverished already poor public services and institutions, leading to either their closure or privatization, raising the unemployment rate and catalysing a wave of migration from Puerto Rico to the United States mainland.[3]

As I was told, Maria crystallized Puerto Rico's lack of sovereignty and its dependency and colonial relationship to the United States. It is no coincidence, then, that in the interviews I conducted with Puerto Ricans, words such as 'unleashed neoliberalism' and 'colony' coloured the conversation, and the word 'exodus' was often used to explain the landscape of vacancy and abandonment – it is estimated that 24 per cent of Puerto Rico's housing stock stands vacant.[4]

It is within this context that Sofía and *La Maraña,* a non-profit organization she co-founded in 2014, began to join and support communities to 'activate' abandoned urban spaces in San Juan. In this way, Sofía became part of a web of actors that have found the appropriation of abandoned urban spaces to be a stark form of political action that challenges established power dynamics and that can help mobilize communities to pursue social justice by confronting entrenched processes of urbanization.

Based on a narrative inquiry, this article presents the stories of four women who are, individually and collectively, appropriating vacant and abandoned urban spaces, physically transforming them, providing them with new uses, while unleashing other processes that have the potential to lead to profound systemic transformations. Building on these stories, the article discusses the notion of appropriation, utilizing Henri Lefebvre's writings. The key argument of the article is that, through the appropriation of these urban spaces, these women are asserting their right to the city and their right to challenge and participate in the processes of urbanization.

In the following sections of this article, I will first provide a brief definition of Lefebvre's notion of appropriation. Then I will describe the research methodology and explain the meaning of narrative in this research. Subsequently, I will narrate the stories of Michelle, Omayra, Marina and Sofía, four Puerto Rican women appropriating urban spaces, and reveal how their stories became entangled on a vacant plot, disentangled across the city of San Juan, and how their actions unleashed other processes. To conclude, I link these stories to Lefebvre's notion of appropriation, draw connections to similar stories emerging elsewhere, and lay out possible paths for future research.

## Appropriation According to Lefebvre

To appropriate something means to take it 'for one's use, typically without the owner's permission'.[5] To understand appropriation in Lefebvrian terms, it is first necessary to comprehend what that *something* that is to be appropriated is – which is an abstract space.

According to Henri Lefebvre, abstract space is the social space produced under contemporary forms of capitalism.[6] Space has become 'concrete abstraction', the likes of exchange value, commodity, money and capital – at once the spaces of consumption and the consumption of space.[7] At the same time, it is the product of the fusion of knowledge and power resulting in the flattened, dispersed, divided and segregated space envisioned by architects and city planners, such as Le Corbusier and Haussmann in Europe.[8] Abstract space is the 'container ready to receive fragmentary contents', the functionalist architecture of modernity produced by abstract labour for abstract users.[9] It is a contradictory, fragmented, homogeneous and hierarchical space asserted through violence and domination over nature and the body, its time and its rhythms.[10]

In the contradictions of abstract space, however, the emergence of a differential space is rendered possible. A differential space is a political project through which the right to the city – 'a demand for political and aesthetic appropriation of space' – is asserted.[11] While 'abstract space is founded on domination', the creation of a differential space requires appropriation.[12] Therefore, a differential space 'relies upon the active agency of the inhabitants [and] a massive intervention of personal and collective uses of space'.[13]

In Lefebvrian terms, appropriation can be understood as a potentially emancipatory praxis that, Lefebvre argues, would 'fall to women to achieve'.[14] Appropriation is a practice that requires an 'active and creative transformation of urban life'.[15] It 'implies time (or times), rhythm (or rhythms), symbols, and a practice'.[16] Appropriation culminates in a differential space that, in contrast to abstract space, 'nurtures differences and particularities' and helps restore the relationship between the body and space.[17]

**Methodological Considerations**

This article is based on a qualitative and inductive narrative inquiry that studies 26 cases of temporary appropriations of vacant and abandoned urban spaces across Latin America, including Argentina, Colombia, Mexico, Panama, Peru and Puerto Rico. Here, narrative is defined as:

> *Everyday storytelling [in which] a speaker connects events into a sequence that is consequential for later action and for the meanings that the speaker wants listeners to take away from the story. Events perceived by the speaker as important are selected, organised, connected, and evaluated as meaningful.*[18]

Textual and visual data were collected from an array of online sources, such as websites of the grassroots' organizations, reports, social media, online news, blogs, online videos, academic articles and conference proceedings.[19] Subsequently, fourteen online in-depth narrative interviews were conducted with the main actors behind each case – some responsible for more than one case.

Held between 2018 and 2020, the narrative interviews have an average duration of two hours. These were recorded and transcribed *verbatim*. The language of the interviews is Spanish and only excerpts have been translated into English. The interview transcripts were analysed employing constructivist grounded theory procedures and situational analysis. Both analytical tools deconstructed the narratives to locate relationships among the actors, their stories and the cases.[20] Deploying Donald Polkinghorne's narrative analysis, the stories were (re)constructed using the array of online sources as well as the narrative interviews.[21]

This article builds on four of these interviews. For stylistic purposes, I will only reveal the first names of the people involved in the stories throughout the text and disclose the full identities of the four women who are part of the research only in the endnotes: Sofía, Michelle, Omayra and Marina. The four women represented in this narration read and commented on initial versions of the article.

At the time of the interview, these women were between 25 and 45 years old, all of them have followed tertiary education, and all have attended universities outside of Puerto Rico (more information about these women will be communicated throughout the narration).

Thus, let me begin this narration where many of these narratives began: on a small vacant plot in the city of San Juan in Puerto Rico.

**Entangled Stories on an Empty Plot**

Before Puerto Ricans met the forces of hurricane Maria, or Sofía began appropriating abandoned spaces, Michelle and her sister had been transforming a small abandoned plot into an open-air community cinema. At the time, Michelle was a young film director who had recently returned to Puerto Rico from the United States and had just finished filming two short movies in Loiza Street. She thought it would be a good idea to show them there but, due to the lack of spaces to showcase her movies, she settled on showing them on a vacant plot. Initially, this was going to be a one-time event, but the warm welcome of the community and the high number of attendees motivated her and her sister to transform the vacant plot into a community cinema for the next three years. Inspired by one of Michelle's favourite films, the open-air community cinema was called *Cinema Paradiso en la Loiza.*

From 2012 to 2015, every second Sunday of the month, the sisters showed movies from all over the world and of different genres and also provided a special niche for emerging Puerto Rican film directors and artists to showcase their films. Movies were projected onto a white rectangle painted on one of the three walls surrounding the plot. These eroded walls were soon covered by colourful murals painted by local artists who wanted to participate in the transformation of this space.

The community cinema started to generate a lot of energy around it, attracting people from different parts of the city, for all sorts of purposes. Omayra, Yazmín and Andrea were among those who wanted to join the efforts of

Fig. 1. *Cinema Paradiso en la Loíza*, San Juan, Puerto Rico, Michelle and friends cleaning the plot, 2012.
Photographer: © Michelle Malley Campos

transforming the plot. All architects and teachers from schools of architecture in Puerto Rico, these women and their students designed and built spaces on the plot where people could sit, perform and sell their art.

The open-air cinema also attracted Marina, an anthropologist turned urbanist who had recently returned from Barcelona, and who was a 'regular' of the movie nights. She organized a weekly, Saturday morning local arts & crafts' market on the plot. The performers of the National Circus of Puerto Rico, the Plenazo Music Festival, and the Independent and Autonomous Book Fair, were among others that found a house on the once-vacant plot.

The plot was also filled with curious little stories, like the one of an elderly man who passed by while Michelle was cleaning the area on a Sunday morning and asked '¿hay cine hoy?' (movie night tonight?), becoming an emblematic phrase later used to announce evening sessions. Another elderly man used to bring Michelle a list of movie recommendations. 'Movies,' she told me, 'that I had not even heard about.'[22] All these people and their stories helped transform a plot into a collective space, forging the essence of *Cinema Paradiso en la Loiza*.

Three years after the community cinema began, Michelle and her sister, with the support of Omayra, Yazmín and Andrea, started negotiations with city officials to make this temporary space a permanent one. Just when the prospect of becoming permanent was in sight, the owner of the plot decided to rent it to someone else. There and then ended this chapter of the story.

### Stories Disentangled across a City

While *Cinema Paradiso en la Loiza* ended in Loiza Street, its energy had spread to many other abandoned spaces across Puerto Rico and led Omayra, Yazmín, Andrea, Marina and Sofía to start their own stories of appropriation in different parts of the city.

Fig. 2. *Cinema Paradiso en la Loíza*, San Juan, Puerto Rico, performance by the National Circus of Puerto Rico, 2013.
Photographer: © Michelle Malley Campos

**_Taller Creando Sin Encargos_**

In 2012, Omayra, Yazmín and Andrea founded *Taller Creando Sin Encargos*, an all-women design collective that supports individuals and communities to put abandoned urban spaces to better use through temporary and permanent appropriations.[23] Their work is always part of didactic activism in the form of a workshop called *Workshop Arquitecturas Colectivas* (Workshop Collectives Architecture). Since its foundation, *Taller Creando Sin Encargos* has organized two workshops. In their first edition, the team and workshop participants joined the community of La Perla. Through creative activities, they engaged with the women and children of the community to analyse the area together, select three sites, and through a hands-on collaboration transformed three ruins into spaces for children to gather and play. In the second edition of the workshop, the women's collective and the workshop participants joined the community of Puerta de Tierra and a group called Brigada PDT, building together a colourful and functional bus stop.

It is worth noting the creative processes and activities that the all-women collective undertook to acquire resources and engage with the community. In their first edition, the collective organized a brunch and cooked meals to acquire funds for the workshop. They also obtained a donation of disposable cameras, which were given to the children to participate in a Scavenger Hunt, during which the children photographed areas of their everyday life that were meaningful to them.[24] These photographs were exhibited in La Perla's community centre and served to select the sites for future action. Omayra recalls seeing the children's 'little faces' while looking at their work and their pictures and told me 'the love they had towards what was done, it was very special because they [the children] saw how everything came out from them'.[25]

An important part of the workshop is to work in collaboration with communities, responding to their needs and desires. The design is a week-long process called a 'charet' after which the community leader, the broader community and other professors of the universities select the best projects. Selected projects are built together! The third edition of the workshop was going to be held in the summer of 2020 but, due to the pandemic, it was postponed until further notice.

### *Casa Taft 169*

Upon her return from Barcelona, Marina lived opposite 169 Taft Street, which had been abandoned for more than forty years. According to Marina – who has become literate on abandoned properties and the legal jargon surrounding this issue – the property had been left in a legal condition known as intestacy after the owner died in the 1970s and had later been declared a 'estorbo público' (public nuisance). According to the Supreme Court of Puerto Rico, a public nuisance is 'anything that produces harm, inconvenience, damages, or that essentially hinders the enjoyment of life or property'.[26] When a property is declared a public nuisance, owners must demolish or repair the properties, otherwise the state may intervene and 'get rid of such nuisances', usually through demolition.[27]

While the access to the house had been blocked, the front yard was used as a dumpster for several years. Given the situation, a few women in the neighbourhood, including Marina, decided to clean the property and plant a little *huerto*.[28] Marina told me that the little huerto 'marked a moment of inflexion that forced the neighbours to get out of their houses, go to the street, take care of it, talk and get to know each other', while unleashing other processes.[29] Soon after, the women started to 'see the house in another way' and decided to 'occupy' the property and transform the space into a 'civic centre' called *Casa Taft 169*. A few months later, they established the neighbourhood association and registered it as a non-profit organization; the civic centre would serve as a meeting point for the community and space for the women to plan collective actions.[30]

Fig. 3. *Taller Creando Sin Encargos,* San Juan, Puerto Rico, the team of collaborators at the newly constructed bus stop, 2017.
Photographer: © Doel Vazquez Pérez.

Fig. 4. *Casa Taft 169*, San Juan, Puerto Rico, abandoned house, 2013.
Photographer: © Marina Moscoso Arabía.

Over the years, the civic centre has established alliances with different communities and groups, including *Taller Creando Sin Encargos* and *La Maraña*, and, like *Cinema Paradiso en la Loiza*, it has generated a lot of energy around it, attracting other members of society to join. In 2015, a law scholar and activist and his students joined the efforts of *Casa Taft 169*, initially helping by cleaning and painting the house, later collaborating with a Puerto Rican legislator to amend the law regarding public nuisances. Marina and her colleagues wanted the government 'to recognize that demolition is not the only alternative' and soon began a campaign called *Todos Somos Herederos* (We Are All Successors) – Sofía was one of the campaigners and signatories.[31] Their efforts resulted in the amendment of Puerto Rico's Civil Code of 1930, with the addition of the law Ley Núm. 157 de 9 agosto de 2016, which indicates that: 'In the absence of people with the right of inheritance, the municipal government will inherit the public nuisance . . . five months after the University of Puerto Rico has expressed a lack of interest in the property'.[32] After this time, the municipality 'may assign, donate, sell or rent these properties' to non-profit organizations, making these spaces available to them to further develop their activities.[33]

In 2017, *Casa Taft 169* was awarded the ArtPlace Award and, at the time of our interview, the property was in the process of being acquired with the funds that came with the prize.[34]

### *La Maraña*

Before Sofía met Marina, she had been living in the United States studying social movements developing in the Middle East. When the Arab Spring began, she travelled to Egypt and evidenced the transformation of Tahrir Square and became 'fascinated about the takeover of the city'.[35]

Upon her return, she met Edgardo and Cynthia with whom she founded the non-profit organization *La Maraña* (The Entanglement), to help communi-

Fig. 5. *Casa Taft 169*, San Juan, Puerto Rico, appropriated house, 2013. Photographer: © Marina Moscoso Arabía.

ties 'activate' abandoned urban spaces. Their first project was *Parque Estrella*, a self-organized community park on a public space abandoned approximately 40 years previously that had become a 'clandestine rubbish dump'.[36]

Through a process of participatory design, Sofía, *La Maraña* and the people in the neighbourhood began to define the future of the park, and to build it. Different to the process in which the community designs and the government executes, *La Maraña* believes that participatory design 'requires all sectors of society, not only the government' to get involved and to take action. After obtaining permission from the municipality to appropriate the park, the non-profit organization started to put in motion a *maraña de alianzas*, a network of alliances that included the local community, other non-profit organizations, the private sector and various governmental institutions – hence the name *La Maraña*.

**Maria Reorienting Actions**

In the days following hurricane Maria, *Casa Taft 169* became a temporary school for children and a space where the community found emotional support as well as canopies, construction materials, food and water fil ters, among other things. However, Sofía told me that, after the hurricane, she thought that Puerto Rico was in a 'state of collective depression'. Marina's feelings resonated with Sofía's comment. The day I spoke with Marina, she confessed that she felt defeated and that the project of *Casa Taft 169* was at a standstill.

Despite how Maria affected people's emotions, it also unravelled new actions. Moreover, it reoriented the efforts of the groups that were already active and gave new meaning to their work. A day before my conversation with Marina, she and the legal team of *Casa Taft 169* travelled to the mountains to provide legal advice to a group of activists called *Urbe Apie*, mobilizing in the municipality of Caguas. Shortly before Maria struck the island, *Urbe Apie* had appropriated a building with the hopes of transforming it into a community art gallery. Their dreams were cut short by the hurricane, but the space was quickly transformed into a community kitchen. This would be the first of six appropriations undertaken by *Urbe Apie*.[37]

In 2018, before Marina travelled to Caguas, the alleged owner of one of the properties, accompanied by the police, appeared at the door asking the activists to vacate the building. With the support of Marina and her legal team, the alleged owner was not able to vacate the property and has not returned. Today, *Urbe Apie* runs a community kitchen, a community boutique, a *huerto*, a centre of mutual support, a community gallery and a community theatre. In 2020, in the midst of the global pandemic, *Urbe Apie* has been quick to react to people's needs and urged the municipality to provide Internet in public spaces for people to work and children to follow their online courses.

**Final Thoughts**

Going back to Sofía's words, all of the above are 'concrete examples' of women appropriating urban space, asserting their right to the city, inserting themselves in the processes of urbanization and challenging established forms of sociospatial production (abstract space). The vacant and abandoned urban spaces these women are appropriating are the product of contemporary forms of capitalism. Abandonment and vacancy in Puerto Rico are the abstract, yet concrete, spaces that have been produced through violence and domination over people and nature by colonial rule and global capitalism (neoliberalism), via extraction, impoverishment, forced migration, lack of democracy and sovereignty.

However, in the contradictions of abstract space – in the vacancy and abandonment it has produced – new spaces have emerged. On a small vacant plot in Loíza Street, *Cinema Paradiso en la Loíza* was initially appropriated by one individual for her desires and quickly became a collective space and a space for collective action where people became networks and networks became entangled to help one another and others in need.

The community cinema was an inclusive space that demonstrated to others that a different way of creating space was possible. It allowed *Taller Creando Sin Encargos* to further experiment with different processes of spatial creation; it became a space where knowledge could be at once produced and reproduced. *Taller Creando Sin Encargos* transported this knowledge to other areas of the city characterized by ruins and abandoned urban spaces, and inhabited by communities that have been segregated and ignored. The all-women collective joins these communities, works with them to produce and reproduce knowledge through their workshops and creative activities.

The community cinema was one of Marina's favourite places in the city. She was inspired by the women organizing the movie nights and wanted to be part of the urban appropriation. She soon learned the power of appropriating abandoned spaces and, with her neighbours, occupied and transformed an abandoned house into *Casa Taft 169*. The house became a place to plan collective actions and generated a lot of energy around it, attracting unforeseen actors who wanted to be part of it by sharing their knowledge and were themselves inspired to act. In *Casa Taft 169*, knowledge has been used to give power to the people to challenge the violent domination of the state and its mechanisms that continued to foster the proliferation of abandoned urban spaces.

Sofía was among the unforeseen actors who joined the efforts of *Casa Taft 169*. With her team, she engages and helps other communities to undertake their appropriations. Through their work, they have learned that the appropriation of urban space is a political project that requires entanglements, people and their stories coming together to transform the environments around them.

I have chosen to retell these particular stories and create this narrative to underscore that appropriation is a practice that has the potential to catalyse unanticipated processes beyond a particular site and group of people.

A small vacant plot was transformed into a one-day open-air cinema and unintentionally became a communal space that inspired others to take action and appropriate urban spaces elsewhere. Like an unstoppable chain reaction, these secondary appropriations led to yet others, and those may lead to new ones as well.

The stories I have retold also illustrate that appropriation is a process that restores the relationship between the body and space. Sofía, Michelle, Omayra and Marina are not abstract, nor are their stories, nor are the communities they work with, nor the social spaces they create. Through their concrete labour, abandoned spaces become meaningful.

In addition, these stories demonstrate that appropriation is a potentially emancipatory praxis. While the main characters in these stories are emancipated and highly educated women, possibly well-positioned in Puerto Rican society, through their concrete labour, the energy they manage to generate around their appropriations, the entangled networks they help forge and the knowledge they produce in one place and reproduce elsewhere, these women open the door to less privileged members of society, including children, other women and the elderly, to participate in the making of their cities. All of these actions constitute the foundations that may lead to profound systemic transformations that can challenge established forms of power dynamics and processes of urbanization under current forms of capitalism.

In this article, I am only able to reveal a fragment of these stories and chose to present them in a positive light. However, the processes of appropriation I briefly described take many years in the making and, as Marina told me, the actors are constantly working counter-current, because there is little governmental support, funds are insufficient and voluntary work is often scarce.

Furthermore, due to the strong focus on the actors behind the cases, the perceptions or knowledge of other people involved in the projects, directly or indirectly, are not present in this article. For example, it would be interesting to interview property owners, including governmental institutions, to learn the concrete reasons these spaces are vacant or abandoned. In some cases this will not be possible, such as the case of the ruins in *La Perla*, whose owners are unknown, or *Casa Taft 169*, because the owner died.

The cases I have briefly presented are part of a broader movement of urban appropriations that manifest in different forms and may be named differently depending on the contexts in which they emerge. In the interviews I conducted for this research, actors locate their appropriations in discourses related to tactical and do-it-yourself urbanism, placemaking and temporary uses. And, as I mentioned before, the four cases presented here are part of 26 cases unfolding in different cities in Latin America.

Appropriation, Henri Lefebvre tells us, is a praxis that falls upon women to achieve. However, he offers no description of this praxis nor illustrates how women are to achieve appropriation. This article offers a brief description of this praxis, but further research to understand it must be conducted and would strongly benefit from feminist perspectives and methodologies.

To conclude, I hope these stories find their way into diverse communities and inspire them to create the worlds they desire to live in, support all members of society to be part of urban life, challenge established forms of spatial production, appropriate and transform urban space, and, as Marina once told me, become the seeds that lead to profound transformations.

**Acknowledgments**
I would like to express my gratitude to the women who shared their stories with me and commented on the initial drafts of this article. I thank the reviewers and editors for their constructive criticism, which helped

strengthen the argument of the article. I would also like to thank Carlos Machado e Moura, Panu Lehtovuori, Guadalupe Bernal Santos and Yazmín Crespo for their comments on earlier drafts of this paper. This research is funded by the Consejo Nacional de Ciencia y Tecnología (CONACYT), Mexico and the School of Architecture at Tampere University.

1 Nishant Kishore et al., 'Mortality in Puerto Rico after Hurricane Maria', *The New England Journal of Medicine* 379 (2018), 162-170.
2 Naomi Klein, 'There's Nothing Natural About Puerto Rico's Disaster', *The Intercept*, 21 September 2018.
3 Naomi Klein, *The Battle for Paradise: Puerto Rico Takes On The Disaster Capitalists* (Chicago, 2018).
4 US Census Bureau, Selected Housing Characteristics, Vacant Housing Units, 2019: ACS 1-Year Estimates Data Profiles, data.census.gov/cedsci/table?q=Puerto%20 Rico%20Housing&tid=ACSDP1Y2019.DP04&hidePreview=false, accessed 11 March 2021.
5 *Lexico English Dictionary* (2021), definition of 'appropriate', lexico.com/definition/ appropriate.
6 Chris Butler, 'Exploring the Contours of the Right to the City: Abstraction, Appropriation and Utopia', in: Michael E. Leary-Owhin and John P. McCarthy (eds.), *The Routledge Handbook of Henri Lefebvre, The City and Urban Society* (London/New York, 2019), 457-466.
7 Henri Lefebvre, *The Production of Space* (Oxford, 1991), 306.
8 Ibid., 308.
9 Ibid.
10 Butler, 'Exploring the Contours', op. cit. (note 6), 458.
11 Ibid., 457.
12 Ibid., 459.
13 Ibid.
14 Lefebvre, *The Production of Space*, op. cit. (note 7), 380.
15 Butler, 'Exploring the Contours', op. cit. (note 6), 464.
16 Lefebvre, *The Production of Space* , op. cit. (note 7), 356.
17 Butler, 'Exploring the Contours', op. cit. (note 6), 459.
18 Catherine K. Riessman, *Narrative Methods for the Human Sciences* (Boston College, 2008), 3.

19 A thorough description of this process was published in: Dalia Milián Bernal, 'Temporary Uses of Vacant and Abandoned Urban Spaces in Latin America: An Exploration', *Nordic Association of Architectural Research: Proceedings Series* (2020).

20 Adele E. Clarke, *Situational Analysis: Grounded Theory After the Postmodern Turn* (Thousand Oaks, 2005); Kathy Charmaz, *Constructing Grounded Theory: a Practical Guide through Qualitative Analysis* (London, 2006).

21 Donald E. Polkinghorne, 'Narrative Configuration in Qualitative Analysis', *International Journal of Qualitative Studies in Education* 8 (1995).

22 Michelle Malley Campos, personal communication, 29 March 2018.

23 The team of Taller Creando Sin Encargos has grown throughout the years, in 2013 the team was joined by Irvis G. and in 2016 Irmaris S. became a new member. To learn more about their work, see: tallercreandosinencargos.tumblr.com/.

24 In the first edition of the workshop, participants were not required to pay a registration fee. In the second edition, participants were required to pay a registration fee to be able to offer them a meal and acquire materials. However, materials were usually recycled or donated.

25 Omarya Rivera Crespo, personal communication, 23 March 2018.

26 Luis Gallardo, 'Los estorbos públicos en Puerto Rico', *Revista Jurídica Universidad de Puerto Rico* 116 (2018), 117.

27 Ibid., 122.

28 A *huerto* is a small vegetable garden.

29 Marina Moscoso Arabía, personal communication, 6 March 2018.

30 The Asociación Residentes Machuchal Revive Inc. was registered on 16 October 2013. See: opencorporates.com/companies/pr/331376-121.

31 More information regarding the campaign is available at facebook.com/todossomosherederos/?ref=page_internal. The list of signatures is publicly available at casataft169.files.wordpress.com/2016/07/cartaalgobernadorfinal_suscribientes1.pdf.

32 Gallardo, 'Los estorbos públicos', op. cit. (note 26), 150.

33 Marina Moscoso Arabía, 'Carta Abiertal al Gobernador', *Casa Taft 169* (blog), 2016, casataft169.com/2016/07/18/carta-abierta-al-gobernador/.

34 The prize was publicly announced in the official Artplace website, see: artplaceamerica.org/blog/casa-taft-169-groundbreaking-grassroots-solutions-puerto-rico.

35 Sofía Unanue, personal communication, 21 February 2018. For more information about La Maraña, visit: lamarana.org/.

36 Ibid.

37 For more information about the efforts of Urbe Apie, visit: urbeapie.com/.

*THE ELEMENTS OF THE HOUSE*

The house is the junction of
dreams
illusions
death
birth
mutations
feasts
contemplation
rituals
conflicts
confrontations
destruction
execution
love
hate
fury
memory
desires
wounds
satisfaction
paralysis
intimacy
distance
ecstasy
mourning
density
absurdity
resurrection
contentment
lust
sleep
wakening
coldness
flesh
the morning
the day
the night
light
anticipation
the spring
the winter
the summer
the autumn
fire
ice
water
earth
flames
mountains
abysses
metamorphosis
flowers
odors
spices
clouds
stones
rivers
the wind
the sun
the stars
the moon
the soft
the metallic
the stony
the woody
the glassy
the crystalline
gestures
faces
movement
penetration
openings
burials
isolation
protection
wombs
walls
intestines
spheres
cubes
voids
squares
transparencies
transcendence
plains
depressions
erections
the skies
the subterranean
the horizon
infinity

R.A., *New York, 1972*

Fig.1. Poem by Raimund Abraham Source: Brigitte Groihofer (ed.), *Raimund Abraham: [Un]built* (Vienna/New York, 1996), 62.

# *The Concept of Appropriation in Collective Housing Design*
# Understanding Dwelling as a Poetic Practice

**Nevena Novaković**

### Dwelling and a Collective Form

The enthusiasm of the twentieth-century architecture debate on housing evokes nostalgia. The relation between space and privacy, collectivism, emancipation, identification (to name just a few), were discussed extensively and in detail. This essay is motivated by a sense of emptiness where architecture theory or even the philosophy of housing design previously existed. An illustrative example of this thesis is the contemporary architecture culture in Bosnia and Herzegovina, where the lack of theory is followed by an extensive production of collective housing, dominated by the demands of the housing market economy, marginalizing the human need for meanings and integration in a wider urban environment. In this essay the importance of *reviving* the architectural interest in the appropriation concept in the context of collective housing design is argued.

In 'Preface to the Study of the Habitat of the "Pavillon"', published in 1966, Henri Lefebvre questioned why eighty per cent of the French population preferred to live in detached houses (*pavillon* in French).[1] It was a period in modern history in which the concepts of collectivism and community were perceived as imperative for prosperity and welfare, both in Eastern and Western Europe. If there was a dominant housing ideology, it was oriented opposite to individualism. Therefore, Lefebvre's question could be formulated in other ways: What was wrong with collective housing as a dominant housing model of the time, and not only in France? Why was dwelling not identified with the collective form?

The collective housing ensembles, usually called *mass housing* or *housing estates*, are probably the most tangible result of the modernist approach to urbanization. The general image of the form comes from the neat geometrical composition of high-rise towers and elongated slabs in a generous open and usually green space. The modernist collective form, though completely different in many locations around the world, is nonetheless always strangely familiar. The applied 'compositional approach', as architect Fumihiko Maki named it, implies a properly functional, visual, spatial and sometimes symbolic relationship of buildings tailored individually.[2] It is a static urban composition made with the tendency to complete the formal statement. This thesis resonates with Lefebvre's answer to the question of collective form error, closely associated with the post-war modernist mass housing schemes. Through completeness, geometric rigidity and urban form repetitiveness, the produced urban and architectural space does not lend itself to appropriation, that is, the creative practices of dwelling that comprise the everyday activities and meanings that transform space.

In this essay several writings of Henri Lefebvre concerning the relation of space and the everyday practices of appropriation, understood as the essence of dwelling, are interpreted. It offers two methodological readings of the appropriation concept in the context of collective housing design. The first is a reminder of the explanation of dwelling as the practice of human self-realization through space. In its context, the collective form is beyond the spatial resolution but enables the beginning of the creative act of space modifications that allows people to feel at home. The second is rendering the appropriation concept as the conceptual tool for reading the existing dwelling space transformation done by residents. It is about learning through appropriation narratives about the space affordances for the physical and emotional claiming of dwelling space.

**Dwelling Is Not a Function**

Henri Lefebvre's studies on the dwelling are associated with the research of the Institut de Sociologie Urbaine in Paris (ISU),[3] but also with close encounters with architects, planners and artists during the 1960s and 1970s. The research that the Institute carried out considered interesting thematic dichotomies, such as the relation of everyday life and urbanization processes. It resulted in a large number of publications of great scientific influence, such as the *L'Habitat pavillonnaire* of 1966.[4] In his in-depth research on Lefebvre, Łukasz Stanek points out that the ISU studies on dwelling were important to Lefebvre's development of the theory of the production of space.[5] Moreover, they were important in his understanding of the production of space as not limited to the domain of bureaucrats and planners, but as also taking place in everyday human practices.

The ISU studies on dwelling in detached houses and collective housing were closely related to modernist architecture culture and the planning practice embraced by the state. Lefebvre was critical of functionalist urbanism, seen through the pre-war Congrès Internationaux d'Architecture Modern (CIAM) ideology of the functional city and its post-war technocratic application. His position is clearly explained in the publication *Utopie expérimentale: Pour un nouvel urbanisme* of 1961.[6] The text is about his reading of the project of the new modern city for 30 000 inhabitants in the Furttal Valley, near Zurich.

According to Łukasz Stanek's research, Lefebvre saw a double error in the design approach to this project. On the one hand, he considered the sociological theory of universal human needs, integrated operatively in the design, as simplified. The list of human needs presented was contradictory to his understanding of the dialectical nature of needs, which are specific to a particular social and cultural group but are by no means the sum of the needs of individual group members. For example, the need for security implies the need for the unforeseen, the need for information also means the need for surprise, and the need for privacy implies the need for numerous social contacts.[7]

On the other hand, Lefebvre was critical about the relation between the sociological theory of needs and the spatial organization of the project design.[8] It was based on the literal transposing of the list of twelve human needs to the seven levels of a sociospatial organization. This approach implied that the correspondence of hierarchical organization of space to specific social groups would lead to the satisfaction of universal human needs. For Lefebvre, each of these levels of space, such as the neighbourhood and district, articulated the technocratic abstraction of space that is supposed to contain social life like an empty box.

In the famous text 'A City Is Not a Tree', Christopher Alexander explained the functionalist organization of the city in a very similar manner. Pointing to the sociospatial totality brought about by the hierarchy of levels, the 'tree structure' was described: a branched mathematical structure in which 'no piece of any unit is ever connected to other units, except through the medium of that unit as a whole'.[9] Alexander emphasized the absence of urban richness and complexity caused by the neat spatial separation of functions and human activities. In other words, the functional city deprives its residents of the experience of overlap and multiplicity of activities.

Lefebvre referenced Alexander and concluded that the modern city based on the tree structure leads to social segregation.[10] He accepted Alexander's theory as a valid argument against the spatial determinism that rests on the functional zoning and hierarchical organization of urban space. Therefore, it can be argued that collective housing incorporated into the city tree structure was from the outset preordained to fail, due to the spatial separation of homogeneous sociospatial units and to the absence of urban complexity in public space.

**Dwelling Is a Social Practice on Many Scales**

If dwelling should not be understood exclusively as an urban function, and residential space not as a separated territory, what would be a good starting points for rethinking the architectural space of dwelling? Lefebvre turns our attention from formal speculations to the anthropological understanding of dwelling. For the answer about 'a humanly significant spatial order',[11] we should not search inside the form itself. According to Lefebvre, we should be looking into the essence of human activities and experiences that spatial form needs to embrace, support and enable. To conceive the *habitat*, we should be understanding the *habiting*, or more precisely, the dwelling.

In Lefebvre's words, habitat is something of a pseudo-concept.

> *Toward the end of the nineteen century, urban thought (if it can be characterized as such), strongly and unconsciously reductive, pushed the term 'habiting' aside, literary enclosed it within parentheses. It opted instead for 'habitat', a simplified function, which limited the 'human being' to a handful of basic acts: eating, sleeping, and reproducing. These elementary functional acts can't even be said to be animal. Animality is*

> *much more complex in its spontaneity. . . . Habitat, ideology and practice, had even repressed the elementary characteristics of urban life, as noted by a very shortsighted ecology. These included the diversity of ways of living, urban types, patterns, cultural models, and values associated with the modalities and modulations of everyday life. Habitat was imposed from above as the application of a homogeneous global and quantitative space, a requirement that 'lived experience' allow itself to be enclosed in boxes, cages, or 'dwelling machines'.*[12]

In 'Preface to the Study of the Habitat of the "Pavillon"', Lefebvre explains the several fundamental theses of his understanding of dwelling. First, dwelling is an *anthropological fact*. That means anthropological in essence and not in terms of the subject of inquiry of anthropological sciences. The material facts of settling on or detaching from the ground, becoming rooted or uprooted, living here or there, and consequently leaving, are all inherent to what it is to be human.[13] Understanding dwelling as an anthropological fact means that it cannot be separated as just a distinct human activity related to specialized space.

Further, the dwelling is an *open place*. Although there is the general character of the individuals that make up the human race, every society through space and time is characterized by changeable sociospatial relations. Those relations mediate *the social practice of habitation*, such as proximity and distance, closeness and separation, intimacy and estrangement, between the individuals and groups. Therefore, the invention and discovery of modes of habitation must always remain possible.[14] Moreover, the dwelling should not be seen as an individual activity related to determining the small-scale territory. The practice of habitation comprises human activities and experiences in the function of personal self-realization but also *relates to multiple scales* of social processes. The dwelling must be thought of as social practice rooted in spatial continuity.

Finally, the dwelling has a *spatial dimension* that can be seen as 'material habitation' consisting of moveable or immovable objects.[15] Lefebvre further explains that the material artefacts do exist objectively, but at the same time, they are always employed for signifying the relations that mediate social practice. This means that spatial patterns of movable and immovable properties mediate physical relations between people, separate them, or bring them together. They form a social organization of everyday life through a spatial configuration in which we live and through which we are moving. However, at the same time, they represent social relations in symbolic terms. Therefore, the dwelling form is a 'double system: palpable and verbal, "objectal" and semantic'.[16] The relationship between the two domains is important and should be studied.

Lefebvre considered two (utopian) architectural projects eloquent in the context of unity between the architectural and urban experience, and interrelations of social process at various scales.[17] Those are Constant Nieuwenhuys's *New Babylon* of 1974 – the future city concept with the playful and creative human being at the centre, and Ricardo Bofill's *The City in Space* project of 1970 – with its large-scale multifunctional neighbourhood. The architect envisioned the new typology of urban housing, organized by strict rules of geometry and facilitating spontaneous living, choices of modes of life, work and free time. 'Structures at once complex and flexible, capable of rapidly assimilating and even facilitating the changes of everyday historic reality.'[18] The projects share the vision of continuous common space and overlapping places of everyday encounters and unknown situations.

### Dwelling Is a Poetic Practice

Dwelling in a detached house is the closest to what Lefebvre identified as a *poetical practice*. According to the author, this is where modern man has the opportunity to dwell creatively, to organize the space to his tastes and patterns. Contrary to collective housing that is rigid and inflexible, often impossible and always prohibited to convert, a detached house is a malleable space and it lends itself to rearrangement. It allows the family group and its members to appropriate to some extent the conditions of their existence. They can alter, add or subtract, superimpose their ideas on what is provided.[19]

Lefebvre relates the concept of poetical practice to dwelling following Martin Heidegger's teaching on fundamental acts of building, dwelling, thinking.[20] Associated with the Greek word *poiētikos* in Heidegger's theory, the dwelling is creative and productive, and therefore the fundamental feature of the human condition. It is not an accidental form or a determined function.[21] Furthermore, Lefebvre translated the understanding of dwelling poetically to the more analytical concept of *appropriation*, in his words one of the most important things handed down to us by centuries of philosophical discussion.[22] As such, appropriation is the reverse of domination, and it has a dimension of resistance or practising the right to the city.

> *For an individual, for a group, to inhabit is to appropriate something. Not in the sense of possessing it, but as making it an oeuvre, making it one's own, marking it, modelling it, shaping it. This is the case with individuals and with small groups like families, and it is also true for big social groups that inhabit a city or a region. To inhabit is to appropriate space, in the midst of constraints, that is to say, to be in a conflict – often acute – between the constraining powers and the forces of appropriation.*[23]

Therefore, appropriation is the open-ended practice that modifies both the physical and the symbolic components of space. Like any creative act, it has an affective dimension and can be related to personal and group identification. To appropriate is to engage cultural practices, representations, perceptions and feelings at a personal and social level. To dwell is to express oneself through spatial elements and form, activities and meanings attached to space, in so doing participating in the production of space and in establishing the social relations through space. It is a dialectical concept, positioning the dwelling practice as mediating between the spatial capacities of what is given and the cultural significations that are needed to be brought forward.

**The Architecture of Poetic Dwelling**

Lefebvre was not alone in his criticism of modernist architecture or functional planning. Critique and revaluation of technocratic abstraction of space came from theorists and practitioners of architecture, particularly in the 1960s and 1970s. The new generation of CIAM members, known as Team 10, was concerned with grounding modernist architecture in the experience of everyday life and city narratives. The housing projects and theoretical considerations of Alison and Peter Smithson, and of Candilis-Josic-Woods, for example, were immersed in considerations of the human experience of place through movement and associations.

In the same discourse, we could put forward the underappreciated design approach by modernist architect Juraj Neidhardt, who spent his life practising architecture in Bosnia and Herzegovina. Coming from the architecture studio of Peter Behrens and Le Corbusier, Neidhardt developed a distinctive anthropological approach to modern architecture, rooted in dwelling narratives and the housing culture of Bosnia and Herzegovina. The principles of oriental architecture and urbanism, which he found in Bosnia and Sarajevo, derive from the philosophy 'deeply social'.[24] Neidhardt posited the spatial continuity of dwelling by detailed mapping, drawing and an in-depth research of space and everyday activities from the scale of the city to that of furniture and objects of everyday use. The author recognized the function of each of them in the social life of the traditional urban neighbourhood (*mahala*), the principle he called the 'neighbourhood cult'.[25] He turned this knowledge of housing culture and the relation of architecture to everyday narratives to the modern expression in architecture and urbanism.

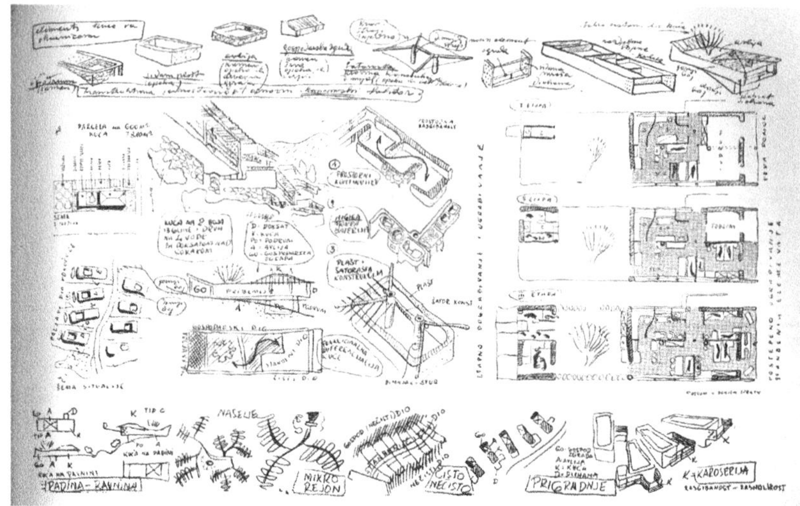


Fig.2. Utilization of traditional architectural elements in modern architecture. Drawings by Juraj Neidhardt. Source: Dušan Grabrijan and Juraj Neidhardt, *Arhitektura Bosne i put u savremeno* (Ljubljana, 1957), 237.

Fig.3. Housing project Koševska dolina in Sarajevo by Juraj Neidhardt, 1967. Photo of a model Source: 'Juraj Neidhardt: Sarajevo', *Arhitektura Urbanizam* 47 (1967), 35-36.

There are also inspiring collective housing designs that considered appropriation as an explicit design method, usually along with the participation of future inhabitants. Project PREVI (*Proyecto Experimental de Vivienda*) is an experimental neighbourhood collectively designed by a group of avant-garde architects in Lima (Peru) in 1960. In contrast to modernist large-scale gestures, the PREVI project experimented with small-scale and high-density housing that was open to future transformations by residents. It was a pioneering attempt to reconcile the conflicting forces of informal growth and top-down planning.[26]

In the same light, Lucien Kroll's iconic *La Mémé* building for student housing of 1970 can be mentioned, influenced by Lefebvrian theory and the Situationist International group.[27] Beside the pioneering co-design approach, the architect envisioned the new living ensemble as an open structure that would support the encounters between the students and the urban environment on a larger scale and accommodate the future modifications needed over time. The approach is defined by Kroll as *incrementalism*. Both examples can be seen as the precedents to the contemporary practice of famous architecture studio Elemental, identified today with the concept of incremental design.

However, it is important to note the very recent research conclusions concerning the architecture of appropriation. In the longer-term outcomes, the quality of the dwelling environment can be compromised by unregulated inhabitants' modifications, as happened with the famous Quinta Monroy neighbourhood.[28] Therefore, the continuity of negotiations of views, actions and experiences embedded in a cultural context is important in the life of the housing community, even after the architectural design process is formally over.

Fig.4. Spatial appropriation of collective housing, Borik neighbourhood in Banja Luka, Bosnia and Herzegovina, 2014. Research on the appropriation of the open space in collective housing was done during 2014. The results of detailed mapping, photographing and questionnaire were related to neighbourhood form and configuration. Photo by Nevena Novaković

**Appropriation as a Housing Design Concept**

Lefebvre's theory of dwelling as a poetic practice invites us to centre architectural imagination on the living body and everyday practice. The design of collective housing can be inspired by the recognition of dwelling as a creative and productive practice of space modelling. In that context, the collective form should be supportive of the appropriation experience rather than imposing other experiences. The goal of appropriation-friendly design is the empowerment of people and communities to project their thoughts, emotions and actions towards the residential space on different scales, and to make a connection with space. This is design that is not oriented only towards the economic, technological and demographic side of the housing problem, but also the idea of poetic dwelling. As the referenced architectural projects illustrate, the idea is not new, but marginalized and underdeveloped for different cultural circumstances.

More operatively, we can define several principles of collective form design, learning from Lefebvre's theory. As a spatial unity, the collective form should not be sharply separated from the environment at large. The porous and ambiguous boundaries of the collective form can simultaneously provide the integrity of the whole and the feeling of environment continuity and the integration to a city territory. In the same context, the collective form should not be composed by only employing built form. On the contrary, the open space is an equally essential constituent of form, providing the continuity of dwelling space to multiple different scales. Furthermore, the collective form should not be associated with only one function or human activity. Form needs to support the experience of overlap, multiplicity, even ambiguity concerning the activities that take place in the space. As a spatial unity, it should not be identified with a distinct social group. The form needs to support the co-presence of different individuals and groups, residents and non-residents of the neighbourhood. Finally, the space that form is organizing should be soft and, in a sense, unfinished. Pliable to creative dwelling practices, to the appropriation of inner and outer space, providing in that way the ambiguity and negotiation of public and private, individual and collective.

In addition, the theory of appropriation can be considered as an analytical theory. That means it can be translated into analytical concepts for identification and interpretation of spatial modifications, including the open space between the buildings. It is possible to create architectural representation methods for the most straightforward and easily observable forms that occur in residential spaces on different scales. Information about what is transformed and how, of transformation position and scale, can be used for rethinking the collective form configuration, specifically and in general.

Most of the collective housing ensembles built dominantly in the 1970s in Bosnia and Herzegovina have never undergone an urban and architectural renewal. They are a legacy of large-scale social effort to meet the urgent demand for quality housing in former Yugoslavian cities. Now 50 to 60 years old, they also stand for the beauty and unattractiveness of modernist endeavours, the joy and unsatisfied needs of their residents. Their peculiarities derive from the blending of the original large-scale design and the accumulation of small-scale traces of inhabitation. These collective housing ensembles necessitate renewal and adaptation to new requirements, but also the appreciation of their diverse architectural values. Nevertheless, they are rich in appropriation and from them we can learn to design and build new poetic neighbourhoods.

1 Henri Lefebvre, 'Preface to the Study of the Habitat of the "Pavillon"', in: Stuart Elden, Elizabeth Lebas and Eleonore Kofman (eds.), *Henri Lefebvre: Key Writings* (New York, 2003), 130-133.

2 Fumihiko Maki, *Investigations in Collective Form* (Saint Louis, MO, 1964), 6.

3 Lefebvre was a cofounder of the Institute in 1963 and its president until 1973. Its contemporary successor is Le Centre de recherche sur l'habitat (CRH), currently located at the École Nationale Supérieure d'Architecture de Paris-Val de Seine.

4 Le Centre de Recherche sur l'Habitat (CRH), crh.archi.fr/spip.php?page=inc-english&lang=en&id_article=13.

5 Łukasz Stanek, *Henry Lefebvre on Space: Architecture, Urban Research and the Production of Theory* (Minneapolis/London: University of Minnesota Press, 2011).

6 Henri Lefebvre, 'Utopie expérimentale: pour un nouvel urbanisme', *Revue française de sociologie* 2-3 (1961), 191-198.

7 Stanek, *Henry Lefebvre on Space*, op. cit. (note 5), 101.

8 Lefebvre cited in: ibid., 95.

9 Christopher Alexander, 'A City Is Not a Tree', in: Michael W. Mehaffy (ed.), *A City Is Not a Tree: 50th Anniversary Edition* (White Salmon, WA: Sustasis Press, 2016 [1965]), 10.

10 Stanek, *Henry Lefebvre on Space*, op. cit. (note 5), 105.

11 Maki, *Investigations*, op. cit. (note 2), 29.

12 Henri Lefebvre, *Urban Revolution*, translated by Robert Bononno (Minneapolis: University of Minnesota Press, 2003 [1970]), 81.

13 Lefebvre, 'Preface', op. cit. (note 1), 123.

14 Ibid., 124.

15 Ibid.

16 Ibid., 126.

17 Kuch Upendra Patel, *Realizing Henri Lefebvre: Ideas of Social Space in Lucien Kroll's La Mémé, Brussels 1969-1972 and Bernard Tchumi's Parc De La Villette, Paris 1982-1987* (PhD dissertation, University of Michigan, 2016), available online at: deepblue.lib.umich.edu › handle › kshpatel_1.

18 Ricardo Bofill web page: ricardobofill.com/projects/city-in-the-space/.

19 Lefebvre, 'Preface', op. cit. (note 1), 130.

20 Ibid., 122.

21 Ibid.

22 Ibid., 130.

23 Lefebvre cited in: Stanek, *Henry Lefebvre on Space*, op. cit. (note 5), 87.

24 Dušan Grabrijan and Juraj Neidhardt, *Arhitektura Bosne i put u savremeno* (Ljubljana: Državna založba Slovenije, NR Bosna i Hercegovina, NR Slovenija, 1957), 150.

25 Ibid., 56.

26 Architectuul web page: architectuul.com/architecture/previ.

27 Patel, *Realizing Henri Lefebvre*, op. cit. (note 17).

28 David O'Briena and Sandra Carrasco, 'Contested Incrementalism: Elemental's Quinta Monroy Settlement Fifteen Years On', *Frontiers of Architectural Research* 10 (2021), 263-273.

# *Narrating the Urban Fabric of our Historical Towns*

**Juan A. García-Esparza**

Based on a research project that involved 'ordinary' objects of minor villages and towns from the Valencia Region, this article will explore informal expressions of cultural heritage in historical towns, and analyse new forms of appraisal in historical urban settlements. Furthermore, it will challenge idealistically constructed scenarios of the past, and provide space for new interpretations on the cultural diversity of informal construction. In doing so, it will also examine how historical values can better incorporate past and present anthropological 'informalities' by discussing how assessment of these artefacts can improve a person's experience of their own town.

## Everyday Objects as Cultural Expression

Reflecting on how we recognize cultural expressions may help in understanding how people integrate, appropriate and provide meaning to places. In historical cities, all types of objects are subject to scrutiny, such as masonry, carpentry, tools and machinery. Most of these objects were designed for interaction between individuals and places, and details of their construction speak of a continuous dialogue between time and place. Materials can be attractive or informative, but in both cases they communicate memories and events, and appeal to psychological wellbeing because they help satisfy intellectual and emotional appreciations – and appropriations – of space. This investigation of informal, everyday objects and habits in heritage practices addresses what has been called the 'heritage conservation paradox'.[1]

The conservation paradox draws attention to how the preservation of historical values often fails to incorporate past and present human-made 'informalities'. Following scholars in this milieu, such as Pereira and Bandarin,[2] one can see the difficulty in confronting preservation with informal historical and contemporary values, and more specifically with emergent cultural expressions, objects and structures that transform the spaces in question. In line with this research, international organizations call for more careful conservation processes through planning and management that pays attention to the everyday lives of local communities. Today, more and more heritage conservation entails reflecting upon previous inconsistencies, integrating contemporary values and perceptions, and developing approaches that are more inclusive and forward-looking in scope.[3] This more permeable form of conservation has been previously analysed by Gibson and Pendlebury, referring to the need for autocentricity and questioning established principles of heritage management.[4]

With this new way of thinking, 'traditional' communities have approached and adapted their respective cultures. They have done so by allowing varied interpretations of 'tradition', assimilating in various ways, absent of polarizing heritage discourses or ideological drives.[5] The historical site concept emerged in the 1970s with UNESCO charters on the 'colonial' appropriation of cultural spaces, emphasizing the importance of sites' historical value.[6] At the beginning of the twenty-first century, this discourse began changing through critical heritage studies, which instead favoured anthropological interpretations that help scrutinize how behaviour confers character to a place where hosts, guests and intruders coinhabit and coproduce informal or 'unauthorized' spaces.[7] This perspective encourages understanding and integrating social values of traditional communities in contemporary heritage-making. It does so precisely because it comes with particular interpretations, ideas, behaviours, expressions and adaptations that result in characteristic experimentations that favour critical – and perhaps parallel – forms of conservation.[8]

**Integration and the Historical City**

As a heritage practitioner and researcher, I am interested in the minutiae of the 'urban fabric' and in questioning how people perceive and experience the physical elements that compose their historically built environments, as well as how to integrate them as part of their everyday culture. By interrogating fundamental principles of heritage management practices, fresh questions about other values and perceptions arise, such as: What kind of integration do we desire, if it proves to be political, economic, social and cultural as well? What integration do we permit or accommodate? What sort of integration do we live in? Do we seek integration in conservation?'

I consider integration a behavioural quality of the environment, which implies accepting, adapting and transforming the place. This includes others' ideas and alternative forms of expression.[9] Contextualizing integration in the world of the arts can help clarify the discourse. Artistic integration might be better understood as something that seeks to open up the perspective of a particular expression, fostering greater understanding and appreciation under a cohesive, broader aesthetic sense. In the realm of cultural heritage, critical appraisals consider alternative values that integrate a plurality of meaning, expression, utility and transformation – creating space for more democratic selection processes.[10]

Heritage practitioners and academics alike now consider the necessity of preserving tangible traces of history in tandem with intangible manifestations of emotions, power imbalances and desires for justice.[11] While in theory these open approaches are meant to stimulate integration, it is still challenging to achieve integration in fieldwork. Likewise, contemporary discourses, practices and uses of historical cities all question how to coexist with previous conservation paradigms, which revolve around contemporary adaptations of historical settlements.[12] Urban legacies and the role they play today still intersect, and clash, with communal wellbeing, knowledge, culture and creativity within what scholars regard in theory as potential spaces for reinterpretation/evidence of ways of coinhabitation.[13] In practice, however, heritage sites are still characterized by processes that segregate them temporally or physically from the previously mentioned expressions (Fig. 1).

Thus, contemporary culture-making in heritage sites is in the precarious position of subjugation when trying to overcome dominant policies and 'mainstream' cultural powers. This balance determines the extent to which integration, appropriation and 'meaning' can be effective forms in selecting and assimilating alternative 'legacy' in ethical construction. The now more open general discourse accepts that the spontaneous, the humble and the flamboyant in the urban fabric may be understood as social expressions,[14] and encourages certain forms of cultural coexistence and cohabitation. It revolves around the relevance and inclusion of lesser-known forms of heritage, which were completely excluded until now. Theoretical discourse now accepts the importance of these alternative values, the values that individuals and communities have always had when adapting and inhabiting a space.[15] Nonetheless, in practice, these lesser-known forms are not yet considered relevant, and still defy the established canon, as well as the prevailing methods, discourses, concepts and practices of heritage studies.

## A Method for Integrative Appraisal of Built Heritage

To discuss how a more open, inclusive and forward-looking approach to heritage could work, the following paragraphs include some findings of the

Fig. 1. Functional integration. Adopted several decades ago, metal shutters are part of a consolidated landscape. While their owners cannot do without them, for others, these are controversial because they disfigure the historical environment's integrity. Image: Juan A. García-Esparza, 2019. Chair of Historical Centres and Cultural Routes, Spain

research project *Writing Historical Centres. Dynamics of Contemporary Construction in Spanish World Heritage Cities*. A team of researchers in Spain is currently conducting this study on the assessment of cultural preservation in heritage sites. The evaluation of the urban fabric focuses on the tangible and intangible characteristics of minor towns such as Ávila, Cuenca, Salamanca, Segovia and Toledo to help scrutinize past and contemporary practices that do not follow 'authorized' discourses in a World Heritage context.[16] The project is still ongoing and will last two more years. Our study aligns with Rodney Harrison, who developed a dialogical model focused on examining the relationship between heritage and other social and environmental issues.[17] This model intends to include fields of inquiry at all levels.

In the context of this study, which looks into the objects as a form of cultural expression, 'integration' means that objects are created, used, damaged, transformed, appreciated, abandoned, analysed and eventually preserved. This definition conforms to stories of recognition and fascination for these objects, and their perpetual or transitory inclusion in the built environment. In short, objects have a biography that changes according to time and interaction. The everyday life of communities exposes objects that compose urban scenery to all the eventualities of recognition, fascination, oblivion and re-enactment. Furthermore, all these objects within the world of architecture are connected with spontaneous exchange of expressions, accounting for the behavioural patterns of communities in urban spaces.

Thus, accounting for these sorts of informal biographies is a matter of researching the plurality within society. 'Plurality' here refers to the multiple biographies of objects that satisfy the different perspectives of different inhabitants. Understanding the significance of places also means understanding how visually recognizing objects contributes to psychological wellbeing, linking the scenery to past and present. Accordingly, following the research, our fieldwork entailed studying objects in relation to their practical purpose, investigating past and present forms of inhabitation. We attuned ourselves to ethnographic methods, in order to better understand activities and objects through which we experience life and place.[18] Consequently, the project merged aspects of sociology, cultural studies and anthropology, and science and technology.[19]

Most of the methods employed, such as observation, interviews, planning and training, offered a more comprehensive understanding of the place's character. In each town under analysis over three years, we conducted annual informative meetings, photo-gathering workshops and heritage days. These activities served to investigate, through cataloguing and mapping, how everyday social practices informed the transformation of objects – and vice versa. Public participation allowed researchers to generate maps that might better reflect the knowledge, quality and intensity of values of heritage. The research method used to include these cultural and social complexities had the following phases: first, involvement with local participants; second, co-definition of architectural and social values with communities; third, cohesion and integration of perspectives; and fourth, creative and sustainable conservation. These four phases resulted in evaluations that enhanced senses of openness and community, and emphasized collective and popular dimensions of heritage (Fig. 2).

The researchers investigated the urban fabric to identify the factors that affect its present form. During workshops, stakeholders discussed their interpretations and ideas associated with defining values. Once defined, other groups related these values to the urban landscape by observing and cataloguing the physical elements that provided meaning for them. Participation of local inhabitants in the conceptualization looked to ensure an inclusive appraisal that better focused divergences towards mutual recognition of values. Harald Fredheim and Manal Khalaf point out that 'value types' differ between stakeholders, resulting in difficulty in obtaining a wholesale interpretation.[20] However, in our case, the researchers wanted stakeholders' analysis to help better understand the specific values of the local character.

Fig. 2. Forms of adaptation and appropriation of space, which to some may seem in a disorderly or chaotic manner. Nonetheless, it represents a true sense and meaning of place. Image: Juan A. García-Esparza, 2019. Chair of Historical Centres and Cultural Routes, Spain

The researchers initially asked hundred stakeholders to determine how they perceived the built environment, but based on that preliminary research, they soon increased the number of participants to four hundred. Photo-gathering workshops and questionnaires allowed the researchers to assess what those elements meant to the stakeholders and how to define the associated values. From the outcome, it became clear that historical and ethnographic values were prioritized. Nonetheless, the evidence demonstrated that the association of intangibilities (such as craftsmanship and trades) to the more tangible elements of the fabric needed thorough explanation, due to a lack of awareness. According to the results, these forms of appraisal need to begin with explicit co-definitions, and to later integrate views and interests.

Philosophically and ethically speaking, co-definition and integration innovates because it goes a step further from previous appraisals that focus on values' cocreation.[21] Other than these earlier forms, this study does not predefine values, but rather co-defines appraisals according to earlier spatial practices – as opposed to those spontaneously created by local practitioners, and later reappraised by themselves in an act of recognition. Thus, collaboration with local inhabitants in co defining pluralities of meaning (phase 2) helped researchers to make sense of local everyday life, and to integrate informal transformations into later recognitions of values through multiple perspectives when evaluating a specific site, street or building that has been transformed over time.

It is interesting how these processes could suggest unpredictable new ways of working alongside, and perhaps clashing with, established preservation doctrines. It has not been until recently that conservation related to how values ingrained by 'non-professionals' can inform conservation studies, and bring alternative practices and objects to the forefront of the discussion. Thus, one could state that co-defining values with local communities is essential to the complex and broad-ranging urban fabric today.

The 'four phases' method can catalyse the preservation of the urban fabric that has understood and respected a plurality of culture. This method's implementation can also provide understanding to how local character can incorporate past and contemporary significance in heritage practices. However, in order for it to work, it also requires proximity, sensitivity and care.

## Conclusion

This study aimed to recognize the realities of particular paradigms by understanding them from an open and external perspective. The project hoped to ascertain how transformations of spaces occurred over time – and how neighbours perceived those transformations as valuable objects – recognizing them as informal expressions of historical and contemporary uses of space. New forms of appropriation and integration of cultural heritage conservation efforts serve as a framework for social and architectural contextualization. The final aim was to value historical and architectural heritage, and people's practices and connections in each context.

The research findings demonstrate that this approach to social values of heritage confronts what conservators have not previously acknowledged as valuable: the unspoken emotional value of architectural heritage. Academic visual analyses, understood as aesthetic judgements, often lacked the methods to engage with the iterations of plurality; concepts closer to the popular appropriation of space. Today, it is recognized that these two forms of valuing space can coexist. There is an increasing understanding that objects in the historical city are complex and multidimensional. Today's objects not only impress us by their age, but also by their ingenuity, spontaneity and beauty. Their meaning can be plural, and open to (re)interpretation. Integrating 'informal' cultural processes into urban conservation thus allows reflection upon the importance of cultural transmigrations in creating lasting structures for cultural capital evolution and values. This study thus appeals to habitats in which such aspects as traditional communities, indigenous peoples and the ethnicities of historical environments challenge the conventions put forward in traditional conservation criteria.

Fig. 3. Other forms of integration in a new urban scene created by World Heritage nomination in Ávila. Image: Juan A. García-Esparza, 2020. Chair of Historical Centres and Cultural Routes, Spain

**Funding**

This contribution was made possible by the project's financial support: Writing Historical Centres: Dynamics of Contemporary Placemaking in Spanish World Heritage Cities (DoCplaceS), by MCIN/AEI/10.13039/501100011033 [grant number PID2019-105197RA-I00].

1 John Pendlebury, 'Conservation Values, the Authorised Heritage Discourse and the Conservation-Planning Assemblage', *International Journal of Heritage Studies* 19/7 (2013), 709-727.

2 Ana Pereira and Francesco Bandarin, *Reshaping Urban Conservation: The Historic Urban Landscape Approach in Action* (Singapore, 2019).

3 Ataa Alsalloum, 'Rebuilding and Reconciliation in Old Aleppo: The Historic Urban Landscape Perspectives', in: ibid., 57-78.

4 Lisanne Gibson and John Pendlebury, *Valuing Historic Environments* (London/New York, 2009), 111.

5 Robert Adam, 'Lessons from History in the Conservation of Historic Urban Landscape', in: Ron van Oers and Sachiko Haraguchi (eds.), *Managing Historic Cities: World Heritage Papers 27* (Paris, 2010), 81-88.

6 UNESCO, Convention Concerning the Protection of the World Cultural and Natural Heritage (Paris, 1972); UNESCO, Recommendation Concerning the Safeguarding and Contemporary Role of Historic Areas (Nairobi, 1976).

7 Juan A. García-Esparza, 'Are World Heritage Concepts of Integrity and Authenticity Lacking in Dynamism? A Critical Approach to Mediterranean Autotopic Landscapes', *Landscape Research* 43/6 (2018), 817-830.

8 Pablo Altaba and Juan A. García-Esparza, 'The Heritagization of a Mediterranean Vernacular Mountain Landscape: Concepts, Problems and Processes', *Heritage & Society* 11/3 (2018), 189-210.

9 Juan A. García Esparza, *Local Character Assessment: Artisans, Crafts and the Historic Environment of Penyagolosa, Spain* (Rome, 2021).

10 Manal Ginzarly, Ana Pereira and Jaques Teller, 'Mapping Historic Urban Landscape Values through Social Media', *Journal of Cultural Heritage* 36 (2019), 1–11; UNESCO, *The HUL Guidebook: Managing Heritage in Dynamic and Constantly Changing Urban Environments: A Practical Guide to UNESCO's Recommendation on the Historic Urban Landscape* (2016). Available online at: gohulsite.files.wordpress.com/2016/10/wirey5prpznidqx.pdf (accessed 24 June 2021).
11 Loes Veldpaus and Helma Bokhove, 'Integrating Policy: The Historic Urban Landscape Approach in Amsterdam', in: Pereira and Bandarin, *Reshaping Urban Conservation*, op. cit. (note 2), 111-122.
12 Sian Jones and Steven Leech, *Valuing the Historic Environment: A Critical Review of Existing Approaches to Social Value*, AHRC Cultural Value Project Report (Manchester, 2015).
13 Mike Crang and Penny S. Travlou, 'The City and Topologies of Memory', *Environment and Planning D: People and Space* 19/2 (2001), 161-177; Mads Daugbjerg and Thomas Fibiger, 'Introduction: Heritage Gone Global: Investigating the Production and Problematics of Globalised Pasts', *History and Anthropology* 22 (2011), 135-147; Tim Edensor and Mark Jayne (eds.), *Urban Theory beyond the West: A World of Cities* (London, 2012).
14 Veldpaus and Bokhove, 'Integrating Policy', op. cit. (note 12).
15 Bjarke Nielsen, 'UNESCO and the "Right" Kind of Culture: Bureaucratic Production and Articulation', *Critique of Anthropology* 3/4 (2011), 273-292.
16 Pendlebury, 'Conservation Values', op. cit. (note 1).
17 Rodney Harrison, 'Beyond "Natural" and "Cultural" Heritage: Toward an Ontological Politics of Heritage in the Age of Anthropocene', *Heritage & Society* 8/1 (2015), 24-42.
18 Andreas Reckwitz, 'Toward a Theory of Social Practices: A Development in Culturalist Theorizing', *European Journal of Social Theory* 5/2 (2002), 243-263.
19 Juan A. García-Esparza and Pablo Altaba, 'A GIS-based Methodology for the Appraisal of Historical, Architectural and Social Values in Historic Urban Cores', *Frontiers of Architectural Research* 9/4 (2020), 900-913.
20 L. Harald Fredheim and Manal Khalaf, 'The Significance of Values: Heritage Value Typologies Re-examined', *International Journal of Heritage Studies* 22/6 (2016), 466-481.
21 Ana Pereira, 'The Historic Urban Landscape Approach in Action: Eight Years Later', in: Pereira and Bandarin, *Reshaping Urban Conservation*, op. cit. (note 2), 21-54.

# *Sites of Narrativity and Spatial Debate* Fences in Neighbourhoods in the Port of Riga

**Dace Bula**

As objects in the built environment, fences are functionally and discursively influential. Aimed at the fragmentation of space, they transmit multiple boundary messages – those of separation, demarcation, enclosure, gathering, protection, etcetera. Regardless of the grounds on which certain segments of reality are set apart by walls or fences, circumscribing constructions exert a discriminating effect on both physical and social space and deeply shape how a place or environment is experienced. Dividing the space into insides and outsides, they create differential regimes of accessibility, safety and visibility. They also produce social discrepancies regarding authorization, entitlement and belonging as well as their opposites, exclusion and prohibition. Border narratives in themselves, walls and fences provide the material surface for various kinds of graphic discursivity. Territories adjacent to fences frequently become zones of space appropriation debates and actions.

This article reacts to an observation that 'as a particular structuring element of urban space', walls, fences and their materiality are underrepresented in research.[1] Based on an ethnographic study of the neighbourhoods around the Port of Riga,[2] it examines people's engagement with fences surrounding the territory of the port. Much addressed by residents in conversation, these fences have served as targets of symbolic activities aimed at claiming the space and promoting dialogue between the parties involved in the formation of environmental relations in the lower Daugava area. The interpretive framework of the article derives from a number of approaches dealing with people's material, spatial and environmental experience as shaped in narration and action – material ecocriticism, environmental phenomenology and narrative studies among them.

**Storied Fences**

The concept of 'storied matter' comes from material ecocriticism, a research trend maintaining that 'the world's material phenomena are knots in a vast network of agencies, which can be "read" and interpreted as forming narratives, stories'.[3] This proposition, in fact, implies two interrelated suggestions. The first is the idea of legibility of the physical world. The other concerns the identification of that which is being read as a narrative. Both notions can be met in the thinking of diverse intellectual trends either in conjunction or separately. For instance, architecture and urban studies operate with a concept of urban and architectural legibility or urban literacy – 'the ability and skill to "read" the city' – advanced by urban theorist Charles Landry[4] and expanded by Klaske Havik.[5] The topic of the 'legibility' of the elements of the built environment (an elevator) is also picked up by Umberto Eco in his discussion of architectural semiotics. The metaphors of 'legibility' and 'reading' used to refer to the interpretive efforts of the human

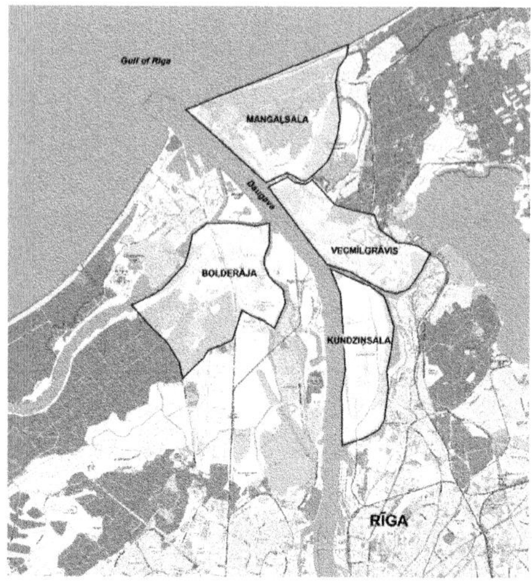


Fig. 1. A map, Google maps, Lidija Zaneripa:
The studied neighbourhoods on the map of Riga.

mind echo a broader idea of the communicative capacity of the material world. Combining a semiotic approach with phenomenological ideas, Eco reminds us: 'A phenomenological consideration of our relationship with architectural objects tells us that we commonly do experience architecture as communication, even while recognizing its functionality'.[6]

In other lines of thought, narratives step in to replace signs, messages or communication. Urban design studies, for instance, speak of 'built narratives', proposing that architectural forms be treated as the 'embodiment of stories'.[7] In environmental anthropology, one can find an idea that 'the landscape tells – or rather ***is*** – a story'.[8] That people not only translate events but also spatial encounters, into narratives or that these are perceived as stories was suggested earlier by cognitive science. In 1996, Mark Turner wrote: 'Action is not the only kind of story. Everywhere we look, we see spatial stories that do not contain animate actors. We see a wall collapse from age, water run downhill, leaves blowing in the wind. These are spatial stories'.[9]

The exploitation of narratives in this and similar ways has, however, engendered criticism. Objecting to a too loose conceptualization of narrative that equates it 'with thought in general',[10] narratology insists on the necessity of making a distinction between 'being a narrative' and 'possessing narrativity'. At the same time, it supports the idea that an artefact might have narrativity, that is, the 'ability to evoke known or new stories'.[11] In accordance with this position is another critique, concerned about the excessive 'proliferation of narratives'; if a narrative lens is used to view physical reality, this supposedly imposes an anthropocentric perspective onto the nonhuman world.[12]

The majority of these considerations imply the presence of a human mind that engages with the meanings of material objects through signs, communication, or narratives. Karen Barad, whose notion of the discursivity of matter is based on a post-humanist attempt to relativize human-nonhuman ontological and epistemological distinctions, uses a slightly different approach. According to her, 'materiality is discursive' in the sense of possessing a potential for 'dynamic articulation/configuration of the world'.[13] Barad writes:

> *In traditional humanist accounts, intelligibility requires an intellective agent (that to which something is intelligible), and intellection is framed as a specifically human capacity. But in my agential realist account, intelligibility is an ontological performance of the world in its ongoing articulation. It is not a human-dependent characteristic but a feature of the world in its differential becoming. The world articulates itself differentially.*[14]

This article, however, focusses on human engagement with the narrativity of the physical world. I treat fences surrounding the territory of the Port of Riga as a 'storied matter', first, in the sense of a narrative subject matter appearing in the interviews of the lower Daugava residents. It is through narrative inquiry that I approach the ways in which these built structures influence people's experience of their environment.[15] In addition, I contemplate the discursivity of the Port of Riga's fences as constituted by their function, enforced or disputed by spatial forms of discourse (signposts, warnings, graffiti) and shaped via symbolic activities of the involved parties, which both address place-appropriation issues and transform the communicative character of these spatial objects.

## Neighbourhoods and Fences

'You cannot get anywhere, there are fences all over' – this is how the residents of Kundziņsala refer to the fact that their neighbourhood has been fully encircled by the Port of Riga. Because it is a relatively recent development, people have living environmental memories and a clear notion of how the character of the place changed with the erection of the fence that demarcates the boundary of the port. 'It was an island!', exclaims Renārs, a lawyer in his thirties, when asked to reflect on the transformations that

Fig. 2. The residents of Vecmīlgrāvis attempting to access the Daugava behind the port's fence. Photograph by the author.

Kundziņsala has undergone. 'Imagine,' he continues, 'it is an island in the Daugava, and you have no place with access to the water! Not a single place!' Kundziņsala represents the most radical case with regard to the impact that the expansion of the Port of Riga has had on the neighbourhoods in its vicinity. In this process, which also involved relocating the port away from the city centre and towards the mouth of the Daugava River, the residential area of the island has considerably shrunk and has been completely fenced off. Only a narrow zone on both sides of the bridge that connects Kundziņsala to the city is accessible out of the previous expanse, which the local community remembers with loving regret.

Though to a lesser extent than in Kundziņsala, walls and fences are influential participants (or actants) in the production of space or territoriality in all neighbourhoods bordering the Port of Riga. During the last two decades, the Freeport of Riga, having absorbed several former maritime agencies, has managed to gain jurisdiction over vast areas of land, over 10 per cent of the territory of the capital, a terrain that stretches along the Daugava River on both banks for 15 kilometres – half of the river's length within the confines of Riga. Even though the territory of the port is split into parts rented out to different companies, it has been encompassed by an uninterrupted border, which is not only a line on a map but has been physically demarcated by built constructions, at times having no other function than that of separating the riverbank from the neighbourhood and thus needlessly ignoring people's attraction to water or rendering it almost illegitimate.

As a result of legal action dating back to the early 2000s,[16] walls and fences have rendered the port's territory isolated, inaccessible and cut out of the urban fabric – 'a capsule' destroying the public space of the city.[17] Interviews testify that city dwellers perceive the port as a closed space and a misappropriated part of the neighbourhood. This can be seen in the way Edgars, a historian by education who lives in one of the neighbourhoods, meditates on the lack of openness and reciprocity in the relationship between the port and the left bank neighbourhoods:

> *The port is a piece that has been torn out of Daugavgrīva and Bolderāja . . . If historically the port was a vivid hub of city life, today it's quite the opposite. And the port's concern consists in a maximum of containers and a minimum of people. Thus, all the development projects contradict the natural interests of the locals. The question is how high the fences around the port will be erected and how tight the restrictions for local inhabitants will be?*

This legacy of territorial planning is also at odds with future aspirations for the development of the capital city, which envisage ensuring public access to waterfronts and port landscapes, allowing people to engage with the vistas of living water and aquatic activities.[18]

**Fences in Narration**

Figuring in the narratives of neighbourhood residents, the port's fences reveal people's place-experience with regard to the perception of inclusiveness, openness and protection. Two contradictory ideas emerge from these stories – the excessiveness and, at the same time, the inadequacy of the built constructions that separate the port's territory from the neighbourhoods. The latter represent the residents' vulnerability and ecological worry with regard to the frequent presence of odours, dust and noise pollution from the industrial operations of the port. Narratives of deficient protection come from homes located next to the port's logistic corridors in Kundziņsala, Mangaļsala and Vecmīlgrāvis, as well as from Bolderāja residents being exposed to the open-air coal reloading, which takes place on an adjacent island. 'Well, they built that fence,' sighs Aiva, a teacher from Bolderāja, questioning the functionality of the fencing of the coal terminal, 'but dust is dust . . . it comes over'.

More widespread, however, are narratives pondering the divisive, restrictive and transformative power of the fence. It is of special concern to the right bank inhabitants, who, from the last decades of the previous century, have witnessed a number of negative effects coupled with the port expansion and relocation processes, such as the expulsion of residents, limiting their access to water, and the loss or transfiguration of 'special places' cherished by the locals. In this context, port walls and fences epitomize unwanted change, a profound conversion of the sense and meaning of the place and, concomitantly, social identities. People who until recently lived in waterfront communities – connected to water by profession, daily routine and leisure – have become residents of commuter suburbs in which spatial movements no longer lead to the river bank, but are halted by a fence. Thus, the port's border walls, even when not explicitly mentioned, are tacitly present in nostalgic narratives recollecting previous lifestyles when 'the boat was a family member', when, having barely opened their eyes in the morning, children jumped straight into the river, when boys spent days and nights fishing on the river bank, when all festivals and family gatherings were celebrated by boating to beloved places in the lower Daugava area. Showing the fieldworkers around Kundziņsala, Gunārs, a passionate leisure fisherman, frames his narrative as a retrospective of a vanished reality and criticism of the present circumstances:

> *Once there was a bus terminal behind that willow. In the front, where you see these containers, we went swimming and fishing, and everyone kept their boats. Behind this fence, there was a canal. Willows grew on the bank of the canal. Now, we basically can't get to the Daugava. There is a small spot beside the bridge where we can unofficially keep our boats, but we are constantly being expelled even from there.*

Boats no longer in use and parked in people's backyards are a typical sight in the lower Daugava neighbourhoods. They lie on this side of the fence while the life in which they were needed has been left on the other, inaccessible, side.

Restricted access is one aspect of the functionality of walls and fences, another pertains to the visibility of urban landscape and has to do with the materiality of the built environment – the materials used in construction. Interviews show how materiality interacts with the narrativity of spatial objects. While modern, transparent metallic fences render port activities observable to Kundziņsala residents, concrete walls preserved from the Soviet times prevail in Vecmīlgrāvis. These prompt stories of an invisible world occupying a part of the neighbourhood and accommodating a hidden life. Narratives of various generations present different forms of interplay between the people, the wall and visibility. Boys' childhood memories recount an urge to see behind the wall, watch the boats, the operation of the cranes and other machinery; they also report on witty solutions to satisfy the forbidden desire. Adults refer to a commonly shared pastime of watching ships and the flow of water; they regret the height of the wall and the constructions behind it, which only allow a glimpse of the bigger vessels and none of the river. People who have had a chance to enter the territory behind the wall share their impressions of a visit to a secluded space, an entirely different locale living its own life of which the neighbourhood is completely ignorant even as it shelters it.

Whether dealing with unwanted seclusion, separation or, conversely, exposure, these narratives stem from bodily and sensory engagement with the urban environment and thus are a telling source for a multifaceted inquiry into human spatial encounters. In line with the thinking of material ecocriticism, they might be regarded as a 'palpable narrative instance of how matter and meaning can enter into a play of signification to produce intra-active relations between the human and the nonhuman'.[19] With a view to spatial elaborations of actor network theory, the stories people tell are indispensable for understanding of how places are co-constituted and co-constructed by 'the flows of ideas, people, and materials'.[20] They support post-phenomenological attempts to advance the 'focus on the subject of experience' by adopting the perspective of the people who interact with the urban space on a daily basis.[21]

**Altered Narrativity**

As a spatial divide and a barrier creating separated physical and social territories, walls and fences inherently possess a contested discursivity. Concurrently, they provide a material surface for a verbal and visual encounter of discordant views emanating from both sides of the divide. Fences in the lower Daugava neighbourhoods represent a site where narratives authored by the Port of Riga and local communities meet, at times clashing and, at others, seeking a dialogue. The message of control over territory, contained by the fence itself and sporadically bolstered by barbed wire, acquires verbal form on scattered signposts (issued by port authorities or tenant companies), declaring a customs zone, prohibiting entrance or demanding special authorisation.

The rest of the border surface, however, is not left blank. The muteness of the wall, noted by Georg Simmel,[22] is enticing and provoking; to use the words of a graffiti artist from Vecmīlgrāvis, Matīss: 'A blank wall is an invitation.' Graffiti is one of the discursive techniques that transform the narrative of walls and fences surrounding the Port of Riga. Sometimes directly addressing troubles that the neighbourhoods perceive as emanating from the territory behind the fence, graffiti produces comments from 'the outside' on 'the inside'. Writings such as 'The terminal will kill us all' or 'Feel the beat!' point at the ecological burden – air pollution, noise and vibration – that the port imposes upon its neighbours. Others, not straightforwardly contextualized, participate in the place appropriation debate in the way graffiti usually does – by resisting 'powers that would inscribe a single legibility on urban space'.[23]

Fig. 3. The narrative of isolation. .

Fig. 4. The green hedge of reconciliation.
Photographs by the author.

Alongside those kinds of competing monologic communication, the narrativity of walls and fences of the Port of Riga is modified by actions that might be regarded as spatial negotiations involving both parties: the port and the neighbourhoods. Recent attempts by the administration of the port to become more open and public-dialogue-oriented resulted, in 2017, in planting a green hedge along the port's metallic fence in Kundziņsala. Coupled with signposts indicating that the growing hedge is an outcome of joint efforts of Kundziņsala residents and port employees, it manifests a symbolic move towards an ecological and communicative reconciliation.

Even more telling and visually impressive are the murals covering the concrete wall in Vecmīlgrāvis, stretching about one kilometre. An activity initiated by the neighbourhood activists and supported by the Port Authority, pupils from all of the neighbourhood schools were involved in painting the mural, and, in the course of nine years, the grey wall turned into hundreds of narratives depicting maritime, underwater and other colourful scenes. The present appearance of the wall transmits a manifold narrative. It tells of the success of an aesthetic action in the appropriation of space – a symbolic act by which space is transformed into place. Creatively attacking the unidirectionally imposed spatial barrier, the neighbourhood residents have asserted their entitlement to the place and the right to speak for it. The port, for its part granting a space for the inhabitants' voice, has demonstrated an inclination towards sharing. The administrator of the port who took part in some painting sessions stated that, instead of separating, the wall is now uniting the people and the port. Those attempts at creating a dialogic narrative, as well as an aesthetic embellishment of dull constructed objects, even though esteemed by the neighbourhood residents, do not, however, address the core issue. They do not contribute to a more organic integration of the port's territory into the urban fabric, opening it up for the city inhabitants and providing a more inclusive public space.

Fig. 5.+ 6. Vecmīlgrāvis' murals. Photographs by the author.

To conclude, the aim of this article was to approach the built constructions – fences and walls – that fragment urban space from the residents' perspective. Oral narratives in this regard are an invaluable source, providing access to the ways in which people experience physical and social divisions created by these border objects and 'read' their boundary messages. Interviews with the lower Daugava communities show that walls and fences surrounding the Port of Riga have had a transformative impact on the meaning of place. Attention paid to the space appropriation activities performed by the neighbourhood residents gives an insight into people's engagement with imposed spatial meanings and their attempts to alter the narrativity of an unfriendly built environment.

1 Joachim Otto Habeck and Galina Belolyubskaya, 'Fences, Private and Public Spaces, and Traversability in a Siberian City', Cities 56 (2016), 119. Less often approached in urban studies (see, for example, Ali Madanipour, *Urban Design, Space and Society* (Basingstoke, 2014), 206-209), walls and fences are a more widely-discussed topic in border studies predominantly dealing with territorial divisions from a geopolitical perspective (see, for example, David Newman and Anssi Paasi, 'Fences and Neighbours in the Postmodern World: Boundary Narratives in Political Geography', *Progress in Human Geography* 22 (1998), 186-207; Elisabeth Vallet (ed.), *Borders, Fences and Walls: State of Insecurity?* (London/New York, 2014).

2 This article is a result of a study in the project 'Living Next to the Port: Eco-Narratives, Local Histories, and Environmental Activism in the Daugava Delta' (lzp - 2018/1-0446), funded by the Latvian Council of Science and implemented at the Institute of Literature, Folklore and Art, University of Latvia, 2018-2021. The oral narratives that constitute the empirical material of the article come from qualitative interviews with the residents (92 in total) of the four studied neighbourhoods.

3 Serenella Iovino and Serpil Oppermann (eds.), *Material Ecocriticism* (Bloomington/Indianapolis, 2014), 1.

4 Charles Landry, *The Creative City: A Toolkit for Urban Innovators* (London, 2000), 246.

5 Klaske Havik, *Urban Literacy: Reading and Writing Architecture* (Rotterdam, 2014).

6 Umberto Eco, 'Function and Sign: The Semiotics of Architecture', in: Neil Leach (ed.), *Rethinking Architecture: A Reader in Cultural Theory* (London/New York, 1997), 182.

7 Crystal Victoria Filep, Michelle Thompson-Fawcett and Murray Rae, 'Built Narratives', *Journal of Urban Design* 19 (2014), 310.

8 Tim Ingold, *The Perception of Environment* (London/New York, 2000), 189.

9 Mark Turner, *The Literary Mind* (Oxford, 1996), 47.

10 Marie-Laure Ryan, 'Toward a Definition of Narrative', in: David Herman (ed.), *The Cambridge Companion to Narrative* (Cambridge, 2007), 28.

11 Marie-Laure Ryan, Kenneth Foote and Maoz Azaryahu, *Narrating Space/ Spatializing Narrative: Where Narrative Theory and Geography Meet* (Ohio, 2016), 139.

12 Timothy Clark, *The Value of Ecocriticism* (Cambridge, 2019), 124-136.

13 Karen Barad, *Meeting the Universe Halfway: Quantum Physics and the Entanglement of Matter and Meaning* (Durham, NC/London, 2007), 151.

14 Ibid., 149.

15 See: Jean Clandinin and Michael Connelly, *Narrative Inquiry: Experience and Story in Qualitative Research* (San Francisco, 2000).

16 The Free Port of Riga Law, adopted 3rd March 2000, envisages that the rented sectors of all companies within the port's territory be securely enclosed and guarded, see: likumi.lv/ta/en/en/id/3435.

17 Alfredo Mela, 'Urban Public Space between Fragmentation, Control and Conflict', *City, Territory and Architecture* 1 (2014), 1-15.

18 *Rīgas ilgstpējīgas attīstības stratēģija līdz 2030. gadam* (Riga, 2014), 67.

19 Serenella Iovino and Serpil Oppermann, 'Material Ecocriticism: Materiality, Agency, and Models of Narrativity', *Ecozon@* 3 (2012), 81.

20 Paul Cloke and Owain Jones, 'Dwelling, Place, and Landscape: An Orchard in Somerset', *Environment and Planning A* 33 (2001), 664.

21 Nima Talebian and Turkan Ulusu Uraz, 'The Post-Phenomenology of Place: Moving Forward from Phenomenological to Post-Structural Readings of Place', *Open House International* 43 (2018), 15.

22 Georg Simmel, 'Bridge and Door', in: Leach, *Rethinking Architecture*, op cit. (note 6), 66-69.

23 Evan Hennessy Carver, 'Graffiti Writing as Urban Narrative', *Literary Geographies* 4 (2018), 188.

# ***Beyond Community*** Inclusivity through Spatial Interventions

**Asma Mehan, Krzysztof Nawratek and Farouq Tahar**

Discussions around social cohesion, integration of immigrants or criticism of the multicultural model of a society are often very abstract, while simultaneously underpinned by some extreme examples of sociocultural conflicts. Interestingly, hostility to the idea of a multicultural society is more intense in places where diversity of cultures is not really present. Living together, sharing the same spaces and elements of (material and social) infrastructure may be difficult and may cause certain tensions, but it very rarely engenders hostility. In this short article we aim to discuss the notion of 'radical inclusivity' as a spatial mechanism allowing peaceful coexistence in multi-ethnic and multicultural cities. We want to propose 'urban radical inclusivity' as a conceptual bridge between discussions around hard infrastructure and 'infrastructure as people'. We see infrastructure as a 'transcendent' element to society, structures created (mostly) by society but that have existed (at least partly) beyond the direct control of society. In our view, once built or created, infrastructure becomes part of nature, as a resource that is interpreted, appropriated and interacted with by various (human and non-human) actors. This article argues against the concept of integration as the main mechanism that allows various sociocultural groups to live together and instead proposes 'radical inclusivity' as a better, less oppressive model of a pluralistic society.

Through analytical and reflective research on the non-cohesion-based approach to integration or inclusion, this article examines the affordances and limitations of integration through various forms of spatial interventions. As an example, we will discuss the Ellesmere Green Project in Sheffield (UK) as a typical small urban regeneration executed in a highly diverse part of Sheffield. This piece aims to highlight the significance of moving beyond the community-as-cohesion model in urban politics and planning for integration.

The concept of integration has multiple meanings in practice, academia and policies, depending on the focus and context of its description. In neoliberal democracies, integration is defined as a fixed and measurable set of requirements for attaining certain civic rights (such as citizenship). More broadly, integration consists of a set of normative assumptions, practices, policies and discourses permanently embedded in specific contexts and directed at particular groups or categories of people.[1] Integration refers to developing a feeling of belonging for immigrants within the host society, seen as a one way process. However, it may also be perceived as a two-way process that enables immigrants and host communities to adapt to each other.[2]

In key works of the founding neoliberal intellectuals, Wendy Brown traces the ambition to replace democratic orders with ones disciplined by markets and traditional morality and democratic states with technocratic ones. She theorizes their unintentional spurring by neoliberal rationality, from its attack on the value of society and its fetish of individual freedom to its legitimation of inequality.[3] For Saskia Sassen, designing a better integration policy means abandoning an array of cherished policies and beliefs about desirable aims.[4]

The integrationist narratives are often defined at the national state level. However, as Pierre Manent argues,[5] the European model of political universalism is rooted not in the nation-state but in three other political entities: the church, the empire and the city. Therefore, we argue that universal inclusivity may be achieved not by 'integration' but by employing transcendent infrastructure (material and immaterial) used by and supporting various users. Integration is supposed to take place between various groups of people; infrastructure is an external entity, making it possible to deconstruct the community and create a new social bond through new interactions between various actors and the infrastructure. When translated into the discussion on political models, infrastructure should be seen as a spatial and material embodiment of liberalism.

Integration in its daily usage primarily serves to denote 'otherness'; however, from a broader sociopolitical perspective, it connotes a problem and process that society as a whole, as well as all of its members individually, must face. From such a perspective, no individual can ever be entirely integrated.[6] The model we propose, 'radical inclusivity' based on interactions mediated via external infrastructure, goes beyond cultures and communities. There is no 'otherness'; there are only various ways individual actors interact with the infrastructure.

In the eyes of some critical observers, the explicit use of integration as a politically and emotionally loaded concept makes it irredeemable as an analytical tool.[7] Costoiu's table of categorizing integration explains models that reflect the variations of meaning of 'integration'. These models are exclusionary, assimilationist and multicultural integration types. Each type is defined through a particular process to be carried out in mainly three domains: political, socioeconomic and cultural-religious dimensions, when integrating communities.[8]

The exclusionary integration model favours the native citizen over minorities and migrants in many socioeconomic aspects such as housing and employment. Assimilationist integration is defined as a process of the assimilation of migrants and ethnic minorities, enabling them to fully comply with the host society's culture and 'abandon' (or thoroughly conceal) their original cultures. The multiculturalism type of integration reflects a pluralism approach to integrating minorities into broader society by granting them equal access to services with the indigenous population. The state even supports minorities in preserving their cultural differences, such as in countries like the Netherlands, Australia, Canada and Britain.[9]

Nonetheless, there is a general assumption, especially within current populist, illiberal democratic tendencies, that the society could be seen as a homogenous whole. 'The people' (often defined in opposition to 'the establishment' or 'elites') always have one united voice and will. The idea of 'integration', however much older, fits perfectly to this vision of society. In the same political perspective, cities are seen as 'contaminated' spaces, where 'the people' are dominated by 'aliens', 'strangers', 'immigrants' or just 'metropolitan elites'.

Lauren Berlant emphasizes that the solidity and sense of our social and political infrastructures – whether nations, publics, labour markets or heteronormative regulations and conventions – are kept afloat by specific constellations and economies of affective investments.[10]

In our proposal of 'urban radical inclusivity' we may follow Edward Soja's discussion on spatial justice. In this sense, the city is seen as an infrastructure allowing the co-existence of individuals and various groups. As Soja puts it, spatial justice is fundamental in urban contexts where marginalized community members are perpetually 'fighting for the right to the city'.[11] Central to this idea is marginalized community members demanding 'greater control over how the spaces in which we live are socially produced'.[12] Followingly, Judith Butler's latest book, *The Force of Non-Violence*, argues that these times, or perhaps all times, call for imagining an entirely new way for humans to live together in the world – a world of what Butler calls 'radical equality'.[13]

The inclusion of particular groups/communities (such as women of colour, refugees, undocumented immigrants and people from underrepresented communities) remains a constant challenge.[14] Infrastructure designed with inclusivity, flexibility and openness as its essential features does not need anybody to be part of any community or ask to be 'integrated'. It does not ask for a passport. Such infrastructure makes people feel connected and related to each other. It makes people part of a whole urban ecosystem. You become 'integrated' by the very fact of using the infrastructure.

**Beyond Community**

By putting forward the idea of 'radical inclusivity' in the context of urban cohesion, we aim to propose a universal ontological framework that can supersede religious, national, economic or ethnic divisions and propose a non-dialectical perspective when discussing social tensions. The aim is to test the hypothesis that the city produces a non-consensual social structure defined not by a collective identity but rather through co-dependence and co-existence.[15] The non-dialectical perspective, partly following Deleuzian thinking, assumes that for every dialectical relationship there exists a broader context that 'opens' this relationship and allows new configurations of actors and agencies to appear. As we suggest above, the built environment and the city itself allow us to understand the process of opening the dialectical relationship more clearly than any non-urban situation. Infrastructure, being external to any community, acts like a non-dialectical disrupter, forcing actors to define themselves against this external entity again and again. Their position is always individually constructed, only partly based on their own values and beliefs and mostly on their needs and living practices. This perspective aims to liberate individuals from the constraints of community.

In his seminal book *Communitas: The Origin and Destiny of Community*, Roberto Esposito defines the foundation of a community as an absence.[16] He does not reject the communitarian understanding of its notion as based on shared identity and values. Nevertheless, Esposito focuses his attention on a violent process of becoming a member of the community. Community imposes on us liabilities and obligations – even when belonging to the community is seen as a gift. The 'coming community' can be defined through radical change and its resistance to imminent power. In his book *The Coming Community*, Agamben emphasized that the future community finds its place in a profound present and within the potentiality of change and transformation to open up a reflection on the idea of 'radical change'.[17]

The problem with community lies in its totality and unification; the community assumes a standard set of features that distinguish community members from those outside it. Each of these features includes a minor mechanism of inclusion that allows the community to expand, preventing its total unification. This semi-transcendent mechanism enables diverse subjects to execute their agency. Our proposal of 'radical urban inclusivity' provided by the city as an infrastructure focuses on individual agency. Here we follow the concept of 'people as infrastructure' as the residents' need to generate concrete acts and contexts of social collaboration inscribed with multiple identities rather than overseeing and enforcing modulated transactions among discrete population groups.[18]

**Integration Politics and Spatial Interventions**

In 2015, Richard Sennett elaborated on the concept of 'porous cities', using Nehru Place, an open-air electronic market in Delhi, as an example to advocate nurturing the complexity of the identity to make more room for diversity. In Sennett's arguments, this is a genuine mixed-use of public and private functions such as schools and clinics and the inclusion of people from different nations and various religious beliefs.[19]

The particular attention to radical civic potential of activism and ephemeral forms of social engagement in open spaces allow different communities with different purposes to be together in space. This is important, if not necessarily novel – many environmental justice activists unacknowledged in this article have advocated and practised these approaches. However, achieving community inclusion is inherently problematic because it challenges society's structure (competitiveness) and organization (meritocracy).[20] Community inclusion necessitates a multifaceted tactic via a broader policy, educational media, public art and spatial interventions. If we suppose that public space assumes rules and conventions aiming to create a society as a coherent whole (coherent but pluralistic), the inclusive infrastructure allows a more liberal/individualistic approach, focusing on individual tactics and uses in urban space. It provides integration by separation in contrast to integration by unification.

As an example, we would like to discuss the Ellesmere Green Project in Sheffield. There is nothing particularly unique in this project; it could be seen as a typical small urban regeneration executed in a highly diverse part of any city.

**The Ellesmere Green**

Located in the Burngreave district, the most ethnically diverse part of Sheffield, this project consists of infrastructure that allowed small groups and individuals to enjoy the green space. Burngreave is situated in the north-east of Sheffield and is now home to people who immigrated over time from different regions of the world, including South Asia, the Caribbean, sub-Saharan Africa/North Africa and the Middle East. Thus, the local community is a mixture of nationalities and ethnicities that manifest their sociocultural and religious practices through various activities in the area.

The Ellesmere Green is in the heart of Burngreave. It is a green space surrounded by many mosques, churches, libraries, shops and restaurants, where various sociocultural, religious, and economic activities take place. Each activity involves a sign of a culture or a tradition that reflects a particular group's background within the community. These activities could be as mundane as buying or consuming food, yet they are essential for sustaining residents' cultural identity. Even the green space is used differently by different community members, as some use it to wait for public transport, some as a meeting point to discuss the political situation in their home countries and others to wait for the call to prayer and sometimes even to pray, particularly during the Islamic holiday of Eid. This has allowed the local community members to get to know each other's culture by experiencing or observing these activities, promoting the spirit of commonality and co-interdependency despite diverse ethnocultural practices. What is essential in this example is the lack of pressure to become a united 'community'. The spatial and material infrastructure allows individuals and groups to do what they please. By keeping spatial and sometimes temporal distances (activities happen at a different time), the members of the various groups do not disturb each other. At the same time, the residents can see each other and sometimes overhear discussions or conversations. The way the space is designed allows them to be together, to be related to each other but not to be unified. A multiplicity of activities allowed by the Ellesmere Green Project helps to imagine radical inclusivity.

Like many other parks and green spaces, one can argue that this particular project is a passive space. It allows various activities to happen but does not 'actively' support inclusivity. But is it really the case? Local authorities led a lengthy public consultation process with the local community when redeveloping the Ellesmere Green, which included the induction of an open market, improvement of the green space and pavements, rehabilitation of shop frontages and the installation of some artworks. The main phase of community participation was carried out between 2006 and 2007 and has been summarized by Sheffield City Council in *the Ellesmere Green Proposals: Design and Access Statement (2006-2007)*. This involved a series of surveys, consultations, meetings and interviews with business owners, community members and leaders. It is important to understand any project not only through its material outcome (building, square, park, etcetera) but also as a process, during which various actors execute their agency.

In this particular project, local officials did not take into account the ethnic, religious and cultural diversity within the local community, as they referred to all non-white community members as BAME (black and minority ethnic). In addition, most people who engaged with the proposed project were white, at 54 and 62 per cent in the second and third phase of the process,[21] while the BAME percentage in this part of the city is over 60 per cent.[22] These data show limitations and issues in designing inclusive spaces. The participatory process always tends to reproduce existing power relationships. People with higher cultural capital, with a stronger position (as recognized by authority) in the community, people who simply have more time to spare are always louder and more engaged in the process. Obviously, techniques are making it possible to overcome this problem in part. Still there are risks, often leading to existing social hierarchies being questioned and the process led by local leaders being rejected. However, even if these data show the limitations of the local authorities' approach in designing inclusive spaces in a multicultural setting, at the end of the day, the space itself, the Ellesmere Green, is constantly created by individual day-to-day activities. It is an inclusive space because the local authorities designed it like this, not because the participatory process has been particularly inclusive.

In this context, commitments to diversity are understood as 'non-performative', meaning that they do not bring about what they name. In the book *On Being Included*, Sarah Ahmed explores the gap between symbolic commitments to diversity and the experience of those who embody diversity.[23]

By focusing on this particular case study, its sheer visibility and limited spatial impact (yes, we can agree that the space does not represent the diversity of residents; there are no symbolic references to any particular minority culture; it is a rather bland, technocratic, 'global' and 'modern' green space, but this is exactly our point!), the space allows new social interactions to emerge. The space provides the platform and means for members of local communities to recognize and embrace the local diversity.

This resonates with Jacques Rancière's understanding of politics as an 'aesthetic in that it makes visible what had been excluded from a perceptual field, and in that it makes audible what used to be inaudible'.[24] The political is a space of potential; something becomes political when it challenges structural (in-) equality issues within the public sphere (which are inextricably bound up with the state and society). The political, then, is situated within dissensus rather than consensus, with the former determining the political heart of radical democracy, integration politics and inclusive praxis (such as critical thought and action).[25] Ellesmere Green is 'transcendent' to all residents and users – both as a place where they perform activities not directly shaped by their religious, ethnic or religious identities and as a place providing 'alien' symbolic references. There is no doubt that a place like Ellesmere Green could be a scene of violence and tension. However, all these potential activities – both peaceful and violent – question narrow cultural and ethnic identities and allow new social relations to be created. In that sense, we argue that Ellesmere Green provides a platform for the incoming community to appear.

Ellesmere Green does not resolve all the problems the inhabitants of these districts face. There is still a need for decent housing, quality education and workplaces. We would like to stress that all these issues are infrastructural. Only structures located beyond the communities but within the reach of the members of these communities have the power to create new, more open and more inclusive social structures. The genuinely inclusive city must be constructed as a political project, where both institutional and built infrastructure aim to achieve social cohesion.

1 Sophie Hinger and Reinhard Schweitzer, *Politics of (Dis)Integration* (Cham, Switzerland, 2020).

2 Jenny Phillimore, 'Implementing Integration in the UK: Lessons for Integration Theory, Policy and Practice', *Policy and Politics* 40/4 (2012), 525-545.

3 Wendy Brown, *The Rise of Antidemocratic Politics in the West* (New York, 2019).

4 Saskia Sassen, *Expulsions: Brutality and Complexity in the Global Economy* (Cambridge, MA, 2014).

5 Pierre Manent, *An Intellectual History of Liberalism, Vol. 1* (Princeton, 1996).

6 Michael Bommes, *Migration und nationaler Wohlfahrtsstaat: Ein differenzierungstheoretischer Entwurf* (Wiesbaden, 2013).

7 Adrian Favell, 'Integration: Twelve Propositions after Schinkel', *Comparative Migration Studies* 7/1 (2019). See also: Sabine Hess, Jana Binder and Johannes Moser, *No Integration?!: kulturwissenschaftliche Beiträge zur Integrationsdebatte in Europa* (Bielefeld, 2015).

8 Andrada Costoiu, 'Migrants' Integration in Host Societies: Modes of Minorities' Integration: Explaining Historical, Economic and Political Factors', *Identity* 2/2 (2008), 2-17.

9 Ana-Simina Sava, 'The Integration of the Muslim Communities in the European Union', *Research and Science Today* 12/2 (2016), 60-68.

10 Gesa Helms, Marina Vishmidt and Lauren Berlant, 'Affect and the Politics of Austerity: An Interview Exchange with Lauren Berlant', *Variant Magazine* 39-40 (2010).

11 Edward W. Soja, *Seeking Spatial Justice* (Minneapolis, 2010).

12 Iris Marion Young, *Justice and the Politics of Difference* (Princeton, 1990).

13 Judith Butler, *The Force of Non-Violence: An Ethico-Political Band* (London/New York, 2020).

14 Anonymized Source 1.

15 Ibid.

16 Roberto Esposito, *Communitas: The Origin and Destiny of Community* (Redwood City, CA, 2000).

17 Giorgio Agamben, *The Coming Community* (Minneapolis, 1993).

18 AbdouMaliq Simone, 'People as Infrastructure: Interesting Fragments in Johannesburg', *Public Culture* 16/3 (2004), 407-429.

19 Richard Sennett, 'The World Wants More 'Porous' Cities: So Why Don't We Build Them?', *The Guardian*, 27 November 2015, available online at: theguardian.com/cities/2015/nov/27/ delhi-electronic-market-urbanist-dream.

20 Andrew Azzopardi and Shaun Grech (eds.), *Inclusive Communities: A Critical Reader* (Rotterdam, 2012), 48.

21 Sheffield City Council, *The Ellesmere Green Proposals: Design and Access Statement* (Sheffield, 2007).

22 2011 Census, ONS.

23 Sara Ahmed, *On Being Included: Racism and Diversity in Institutional Life* (Durham, NC, 2012).

24 Jacques Rancière, *The Philosopher and His Poor,* edited by Andrew Parker and translated by John Drury, Corinne Oster and Andrew Parker (Durham, NC, 2003), 226.

25 Jacques Rancière, *Dissensus: On Politics and Aesthetics*, translated and edited by Steven Corcoran (London, 2015).

## A Walk to the Cherwell River Meadows: (Meaningfulness and) the Perceivable Form of the Urban Landscape

Saskia de Wit

In order to generate insights on the role of perceivable form, this article presents an excursion to Oxford, a mid-size European city with a strong urban identity. By weaving the landscape of the non-traditional architectural ensemble of St Catherine's College into that of the traditional urban landscape, this paper aims to unfold (the perception of) the physical landscape, beyond the polemics of architectural style, as a generator of meaningfulness. Devoid of the style characteristics that determine our mental image of Oxford but remaining loyal to the programmatic and compositional logic of the Oxford colleges, the ensemble exposes just how much the quality of the physical landscape can affect what we perceive and how we attach meanings to what we perceive.

**Saskia de Wit** is assistant professor in the Section of Landscape Architecture, Delft University of Technology, the Netherlands. She holds a Master's degree from Wageningen University and a PhD from Delft University of Technology. She combines teaching and research with practice at her own firm, *Saskia de Wit tuin en landschap*. Her research focuses on the garden as a lens for research into the perception of place, sensory landscape qualities, contemporary notions of nature and metropolitan landscapes.

## Narrative Deserts and Embodied Meanings in the City: The Microstories of Ghent's City Pavilion

Kris Pint

In his famous analysis of everyday life, Michel de Certeau examines how the technocratic discourse of production and consumption deprives urban inhabitants of meaningful stories. At the same time, he discerns a proliferation of microstories that resist this homogenization. We want to argue that de Certeau's work is still very relevant for a discussion about meaningfulness and the contemporary city, if we take into account that these stories can also be antagonistic and even destructive. Following the work of Mark Johnson, we also would like to regard meaning as something that is not only linguistic, but emerges from an affective, sensorial interaction with our built environment. As a case study, we will discuss Ghent's City Pavilion, designed by Robbrecht & Daem and Marie-José Van Hee architects, as a generator of stories and embodied meanings, both positive and negative.

**Kris Pint** is assistant professor at the Faculty of Architecture and Arts, Hasselt University, Belgium. His teaching and research occupy the domains of cultural philosophy, semiotics and scenography. His research focuses on literature, (interior) architecture and visual arts, more specifically on the alternative possibilities of living, dwelling and knowing – fundamentals that artistic research helps to explore. He also examines how elements of creative (non-)fiction can be used in artistic research.

## The Belly of Naples and Displaced Meanings, City-as-Body and City-as-Theatre in Commentaries on the Old Town *Risanamento*: Deconstructing the Stereotype of the Picturesque

Giuseppe Resta

This article considers the formation of stereotypical images associated with the picturesque of the South, analysing the case of Naples. The text examines selected urban images reported before and after the late-nineteenth-century *Risanamento* period of dramatic renovations of the old town, with a focus on city-as-body and city-as-theatre tropes. The inevitable departure is *Il Ventre di Napoli* (1884-1906, The belly of

Naples) by Matilde Serao. We will see how Serao tackles all contradictions of a built environment teeming with life. We have then connected excerpts from foreign travellers, again before and after the ***Risanamento***, to the pleasures (or sickness) of flesh and theatricality. These displaced meanings parallel many descriptions by writers that travelled to Naples: Charles Dickens and the pantomime, Jean-Paul Sartre's delirium of flesh and rotten food, Benjamin and the city-as-theatre – all deconstructing the stereotype of the picturesque.

**Giuseppe Resta** is a PhD architect. He is assistant professor of Architecture at the Yeditepe University, Istanbul, Turkey. He is owner and curator of Antilia Gallery (IT) and co-founder of the architecture think tank PROFFERLO (IT-UK). Resta is a member of the board of directors of ICoRSA (IE). His research on architecture and the city is focused on the relationship between space and power, and on adaptive reuse via artistic practices. His latest monographic books are *AB Chvoya: Architectural Bureau* (2020) and *Atlante di progetti per l'Albania: La città e il territorio nel primo Novecento* (2019), both published by Libria. Resta joined the COST Action CA18126 *Writing Urban Places* for its multidisciplinary approach to urban narration.

## Appropriation and Gendered Spaces: A Discussion on Elena Ferrante's Neapolitan Novels

Sernaz Arslan

Elena Ferrante's series *Neapolitan Novels* (2011-2014) has been characterized as a female *bildungsroman* that begins in 1950s Naples. It follows the lives of two protagonists, Lenù (Elena) Greco and Lila (Raffaella) Cerullo, from childhood to old age as they struggle to figure out what they want/need to be/become by challenging the dominant gender roles and power relations embedded in the society. Within the framework of

Gillian Rose and Doreen Massey's theoretical conceptualizations regarding space, this article aims to discuss appropriation of urban space from a gendered perspective as presented through the *Neapolitan Novels* and in Ferrante's Naples. Ferrante's Neapolitan novels not only portray the personal transformation of the main characters Lenú and Lila, but also, their practices of urban appropriation, their relationship with the neighbourhood they live in along with the transformation of Naples as a socially constructed space itself.

**Sernaz Arslan** is a doctoral candidate in Political Science at Istanbul Bilgi University, where she is also a research assistant in the Department of International Relations. Her research focuses on how rural to urban migrants belonging to different generations experience and practice urban citizenship in Istanbul. She is engaged in generational analysis with qualitative research methods, particularly the narrative approach. Her areas of interest include urban politics and history, urban narratives, spatial participation, gender studies and social policy.

## Narratives of Appropriation: Abandoned Spaces, Entangled Stories and Profound Urban Transformations

Dalia Milián Bernal

Based on a narrative inquiry, this article presents the stories of four women who are, individually and collectively, appropriating vacant and abandoned urban spaces, physically transforming them, providing them with new uses, while unleashing other processes that have the potential to lead to profound systemic transformations. Building on these stories, the article discusses the notion of appropriation, utilizing Henri Lefebvre's writings. The key argument of the article is that, through the appropriation of these urban spaces, these women are asserting their right to the city and their right to challenge and participate in the processes of urbanization.

**Dalia Milián Bernal** is a doctoral researcher and lecturer at the School of Architecture, Faculty of the Built Environment at Tampere University in Finland. Her background is in the field of architecture and her current research focuses on the temporary uses of vacant and abandoned urban spaces in the context of Latin America. Delving into online arenas, following several cases, and applying different analytic methods of narrative inquiry, she aims to explain why temporary uses develop across Latin American cities and unearth their deeper meaning. Currently, she teaches sociospatial aspects of sustainable architecture, critical urban theory and, since 2019, she coordinates the IFHP Urban Planning and Design Summer School in Finland. She is the co-founder of the collective-blog *Interrogativa*, a platform that discusses diverse urban processes through the perspective of women and their experience of urban space.

## The Concept of Appropriation in Collective Housing Design: Understanding Dwelling as a Poetic Practice

Nevena Novaković

The article aims to contribute to the theoretical debate on collective housing design by focusing on dwelling as a poetic practice. More precisely, it explores the methodological potential of the concept of appropriation that fosters the understanding of dwelling as the creative practice of human self-realization through space. It does so by interpreting selected writings of Henri Lefebvre and bringing forward exemplary housing projects. The theoretical review concludes with several principles of housing design that underline the importance of the continuity, overlapping and 'softness' of dwelling space. Moreover, the article conceptualizes appropriation as an analytical tool for reading the transformation of existing space made by residents. Appropriation narratives, in this way, enable housing design to understand and consider the spatial characteristics that contribute to meaningful emotional connections between space and people on different scales.

**Nevena Novaković** is an assistant professor at the University of Banja Luka Bosnia and Herzgovinia, Faculty of Architecture, Civil Engineering and Geodesy, where she teaches courses in the field of Urban Design and Urban Theory. Nevena obtained her doctorate from the University of Belgrade, Faculty of Architecture, in 2014. She was a visiting scholar at the University of Michigan in 2008 and the University of Glasgow in 2018. Her research and scholarship focuses on urban form theory and urban form contemporary research at different scales, from collective housing to metropolitan urban territories.

## Narrating the Urban Fabric of our historical towns

Juan A. García Esparza

This article explores informal expressions of cultural heritage in historical towns. The framework in historical urban settlements uses research to analyse the entanglements of urban heritage when surveyed as environments where subcultures and minorities inhabit and create those sites. The approach challenges the idealistic constructed scenarios of the past and provides space for new interpretations on the cultural diversity of the unplannable or informal in place-making. This paper examines the heritage conservation paradox on how historical values can better incorporate past and contemporary anthropological informalities.

**Juan A. García Esparza** is a senior lecturer at Universitat Jaume I, where he teaches Conservation and Heritage Management. His research interests rely on heritage science in a broad sense, from cultural landscapes to built environments. His current research centres on contemporary cultural place-making in historical towns and villages. He is an elected member of the Regional Committee for Intangible Cultural Heritage at Comunitat Valenciana, Spain, and an associate member of the ICOMOS International Committee for Historical Towns and Villages CIVVIH.

## Sites of Narrativity and Spatial Debate: Fences in Neighbourhoods in the Port of Riga

Dace Bula

Based on an ethnographic study of the neighbourhoods in the vicinity of the Port of Riga, the article examines people's engagement with fences surrounding the territory of the port. It reacts to an observation that walls, fences and their materiality are underrepresented in research. Focusing on human engagement with the narrativity of the physical world, the article treats port's fences as 'storied matter'. This includes, first, an observation that these built structures constitute a narrative subject matter frequently appearing in the interviews of the lower Daugava residents. In addition, the discursivity of the Port of Riga's fences is contemplated as constituted by their function, enforced or disputed by spatial forms of discourse (signposts, warnings, graffiti) and shaped via symbolic activities of the involved parties, which both address place-appropriation issues and transform the communicative character of these spatial objects.

**Dace Bula** is a cultural scholar, currently the director of the Institute of Literature, Folklore and Art, University of Latvia. She has published two monographs (in Latvian): *The Nation of Singers: Folklore and National Ideology* (2000) and *Contemporary Folkloristics: Paradigm*

*Shift* (2011), as well as edited and co-edited a number of volumes. Her research interests and publications include a range of topics, such as history and theory of folklore studies, popular calendric practices, culture(s) and identities in the post-Soviet condition, community studies, and nostalgia; and, more recently, environmental humanities and eco-narratives.

## Beyond Community Inclusivity through Spatial Interventions

Asma Mehan, Krzysztof Nawratek and Farouq Tahar

This article argues against the concept of integration as the main mechanism allowing various sociocultural groups to live together and instead proposes 'radical inclusivity' as a better, less oppressive model of a pluralistic society. Through analytical and reflective research on the non-cohesion-based approach to integration or inclusion, this article is devoted to examining the affordances and limitations of integration through various forms of spatial interventions. As an example, we will discuss the Ellesmere Green Project in Sheffield (UK) as a typical small urban regeneration executed in a highly diverse part of Sheffield. This piece aims to bring forward the significance of moving beyond the community-as-cohesion model in urban politics and planning for integration.

**Asma Mehan** is an author, educator, researcher, and architectural historian. She is a Senior Researcher affiliated with the University of Porto (Portugal). Asma has studied, researched, and taught architecture and urban design in Europe, Asia, and Australia. She is the author of the book *Kuala Lumpur: Community, Infrastructure, and Urban Inclusivity* (with Marek Kozlowski and Krzysztof Nawratek, 2020). She taught at TU Delft, TU Munich, ZK/U Berlin Center for Art and Urbanistics, and Deakin University in Melbourne (Australia). Asma has also authored over fifty articles and essays in scholarly books and professional journals of multiple languages on critical urban studies, architecture, urban planning, housing, and heritage studies. She has participated in exhibitions and by carrying her practice beyond writing to visual media.

**Krzysztof Nawratek**, PhD, is a Senior Lecturer (associate professor) in Humanities and Architecture at the University of Sheffield, UK. He is an author of *City as a Political Idea* (2011), *Holes in the Whole: Introduction to urban Revolutions* (2012), *Radical Inclusivity: Architecture and Urbanism* (ed. 2015), *Urban Re-Industrialisation* (ed. 2017), *Total Urban Mobilisation: Ernst Junger and Postcapitalist City* (2018), *Kuala Lumpur: Community, Infrastructure and Urban Inclusivity* (with Asma Mehan and Marek Kozlowski, 2020) and several articles and papers.

**Farouq Tahar** is a PhD candidate at Sheffield School of Architecture, interested in exploring the social role of architecture and the impact of the built environment on communities' performance. He holds a Master of Arts in Architectural Design from Sheffield School of Architecture. Farouq worked in practice for several years in Algeria and has gained decent experience in academia when working in Saudi Arabia as a researcher/consultant for the Institute of Pilgrimage research at Um Al-Qura University. After years of studies and work experience, he launched his PhD research to investigate the Muslims' participation in architecture and urban projects in Britain, and the impact of community cohesion and integration policies on their participation.

editors

**Sonja Novak,** PhD, is an assistant professor in the Department of German Studies, Faculty of Humanities and Social Sciences in Osijek, Croatia, where she teaches History of German Literature and courses on Literary Theory at undergraduate (BA), graduate (MA) and postgraduate (PhD) level. She conducts her research in the humanities within the research field of Philology and her area of expertise is Literary Theory and History of Literature. Current research topics cover the connection between literature and (urban) space, comparative literature and analysis of the phenomenon of systems in crisis in contemporary fiction and drama with special emphasis on German and Croatian literature.

**Angeliki Sioli**, PhD, is an assistant professor of architecture at the Chair of Methods of Analysis and Imagination, Delft University of Technology. She obtained a professional diploma in Architecture from the University of Thessaly and a post-professional Master's in Architectural Theory and History from the National Technical University of Athens. She completed her PhD at McGill University, Montreal. Her research seeks connections between architecture and literature in the public realm of the city, focusing on aspects of embodied perception of place. Her work on architecture, literature and pedagogy has been published in a number of books and presented at numerous conferences. She was recently awarded the 2021 Teaching Fellow Comenius Grant for Teaching Innovation and she has edited the collected volumes *The Sound of Architecture: Acoustic Atmospheres in Place* (Leuven University Press, 2022) and *Reading Architecture: Literary Imagination and Architectural Experience* (Routledge, 2018). Before joining Delft University of Technology, Sioli taught at McGill University in Montreal; Tec de Monterrey in Mexico; and Louisiana State University in the USA.

**Susana Oliveira**, PhD, is Head of Drawing Department at the Faculty of Fine Arts, Lisbon University, Portugal. She studied Painting, has an MA in Aesthetics and Philosophy of Art and a PhD in Communication Sciences. She published several articles and books on visual culture, and worked on museology projects such as Lisbon Museu da Cidade and Museu do Côa. She co-organized the 1st International Conference on Architecture and Fiction – *Once Upon a Place*, Lisbon 2010, published in book format in 2013. She was visiting scholar at GSAPP – Columbia University NY in 2014, with postdoctoral research in *Architectural Imagination in Fiction Literature*, a subject she continues to pursue, namely within graphic representation and word & image studies. She also works as a freelance illustrator and has published over 25 youth and children's books. She is vice-chair of EU COST Action *Writing Urban Places.*

**Klaske Havik** is professor of Methods of Analysis and Imagination at Delft University of Technology. Her research relates architectural and urban questions, such as the use, experience and imagination of place, to literary language. Her book *Urban Literacy: Reading and Writing Architecture*, based on her PhD, was published in 2014. Havik initiated the platform *Writingplace* and organized the 2nd international conference on architecture and fiction: *Writingplace: Literary Methods in Architectural Research and Design* (2013), which resulted in the book *Writingplace, Investigations in Architecture and Literature* (2016). For architecture journal *OASE*, she edited, among other issues, *OASE* 98 *Narrating Urban Landscapes*, *OASE* 91 *Building Atmosphere* (2013), *OASE* 85, *Productive Uncertainty* (2011) and *OASE* 70 *Architecture and Literature* (2007). Havik's literary work has appeared in Dutch poetry collections and literary magazines, while a collection of her poems in English appeared as *Way and Further* (2021). Havik is editor of the *Writingplace Journal*, and chair of the EU COST Action *Writing Urban Places.*

# COLOPHON

***Writingplace, Journal for Architecture and Literature***

#6 City Narratives as Places of Meaningfulness, Appropriation and Integration

This publication is based upon work from COST Action CA 18126 Writing Urban Places, supported by COST (European Cooperation in Science and Technology).

COST is a funding agency for research and innovation networks. Our Actions help connect research initiatives across Europe and enable scientists to grow their ideas by sharing them with their peers. This boosts their research, career and innovation. **www.cost.eu**

**Editors of this issue:**
**Sonja Novak**
**Susana Oliveira**
**Angeliki Sioli**
**Klaske Havik**



**Copy editing: D'Laine Camp**

**Design & cover:**
**Studio Sanne Dijkstra**

**Publisher:**
**Marcel Witvoet, nai010 publishers in collaboration with TU Delft Open**



This publication was made possible by:

nai010 publishers

nai010 publishers is an internationally orientated publisher specialized in developing, producing and distributing books in the fields of architecture, urbanism, art and design. www.nai010.com

nai010 books are available internationally at selected bookstores and from the following distribution partners:

North, Central and South America - Artbook | D.A.P., New York, USA, dap@dapinc.com

Rest of the world – Idea Books, Amsterdam, the Netherlands, idea@ideabooks.nl

For general questions, please contact nai010 publishers directly at sales@nai010.com or visit our website www.nai010.com for further information.

NUR 648
BISAC ARC001000
THEMA AMA